Making
Wire Jewelry

Making
Wire Jewelry

Martine Callaghan

KALMBACH BOOKS

Kalmbach Books
21027 Crossroads Circle
Waukesha, Wisconsin 53186
www.Kalmbach.com/Books

© 2012 Martine Callaghan

Published in 2012
16 15 14 13 12   1 2 3 4 5

Manufactured in the United States of America

ISBN: 978-0-87116-435-3

Editor Mary Wohlgemuth
Art Director Lisa Bergman
Photographer James Forbes, William Zuback

Library of Congress Cataloging-in-Publication Data
Callaghan, Martine.
  Making wire jewelry / Martine Callaghan.
    p. : col. ill. ; cm. – (The absolute beginners guide ; [4])
  "Everything you need to know to get started."–Cover.
  ISBN: 978-0-87116-435-3

  1. Wire jewelry--Handbooks, manuals, etc. 2. Wire jewelry–Patterns. 3. Beadwork–Handbooks, manuals, etc.
  4. Beadwork–Patterns. 5. Jewelry making. I. Title.

TT214.3 .C25 2012
745.594/2

Contents

Extra goodies

Introduction

WIRE IS A TRULY AMAZING material for making jewelry. With a few simple tools and techniques and a few lengths of inexpensive metal, you can be on your way to making fabulous jewelry that is not only unique and attractive, but also extremely strong and durable. And wireworking doesn't require a huge investment in time: Many of the projects in this book can be made in less than an hour. Making the projects is a guaranteed way to build the skills that will turn you into a talented wireworker: accuracy, patience, and attention to detail. You'll also get quite friendly with your materials and tools along the way.

Take your time and work your wire slowly, calmly, unhurriedly, and lovingly, and you will be amply rewarded. You are about to give a humble piece of wire life, beauty, and function!

As a trained teacher, I am constantly driven by the thought that there is always a better, simpler way of passing on knowledge. In this book, you will find many simple and innovative ways of learning the basics, including quite a few tricks to make some of the techniques easier to understand.

This book aims to get you started making gorgeous wire jewelry right from the start: Each project teaches several basic techniques. The projects are organized in order of difficulty from the simplest to the most challenging, and each new piece builds on and expands the skills learned in the previous one.

I suggest that if you are an absolute beginner, you work your way through the projects in the order they are presented to increase your skill levels gradually and thoroughly. As you progress through the projects, you will become more at ease with your tools and wire.

Be sure to take advantage of "Another Idea"—a variation on the featured project—to practice and develop your design skills.

Whether you have never picked up a pair of pliers or you already have some experience in wirework, you will find this book a useful reference to take you step by step through all the basic techniques needed to produce beautiful, professional-looking wirework. Wirework is not only an ancient and intricate art form, it's also an exciting, challenging, and—I have to warn you!—totally engrossing hobby.

I hope this book will give you the solid foundation needed to be a skillful wireworker and, in the process, inspire you to develop your very own style. Above all, I hope you will have good fun.

It's an exciting, challenging, and **totally engrossing hobby.**

Basics

Your main material is naturally going to be wire. As I'll explain later, many different types of wire can be used in jewelry, but to minimize the cost, I suggest you work mostly with copper or plated copper to practice your technique. The rule of thumb is to make two pieces for practice and one "for real." So, if you want to make a project using sterling silver, for instance, practice it twice using silver-plated copper, and then move to sterling. You will find that, by the third time, you will have ironed out all the problems. Of course, you don't have to use sterling silver at all; copper is a pure material in its own right, and good-quality silver-plated or silver-filled wire will also stand the test of time.

I can already hear you say, "But I want beads in my wirework!" Sure you do! Those gorgeous, sparkly things are just impossible to resist. Fortunately (or is it unfortunately?) for wirework, we don't need a huge stash, as the wire is the main event. What beads you choose to decorate your wirework will be entirely up to you.

We all have different tastes, so there is no right or wrong choice and there are so many hard-to-resist beauties available. However, keep in mind that some of the projects have precise measurements adapted to a particular size of bead, and delicate beads can be damaged by wire.

Now it's time to make friends with your wire. Cut off a piece and bend it with your fingers, make some shapes, play with it, see what it can do. How does it feel? Springy? Soft? Stiff? Let's talk more about our favorite material.

Colored craft wire and copper wire are excellent practice materials for beginners.

MATERIALS

Wire types

Before you start any wire jewelry project, you will make four important choices: metal, gauge, temper, and shape.

Metal

Economical **copper**, a nonprecious (base) metal, is an excellent choice for practice wire, and some people like to use it for finished jewelry as well. Copper wire is soft and easy to work with. Brass and bronze, two other base metals, are much stiffer to work. Copper takes on a mellow, aged patina with time.

Color-coated wire, sometimes called **craft** wire, is inexpensive, nontarnishing, and it gives jewelry a look that's completely different than traditional metal colors. I often use this wire when working out new designs because I can use up great lengths without worrying about the cost.

You need to use a light touch to avoid marring the color coating with your tools.

Good-quality **silver-plated** wire gives you the look of silver without the price tag of pure precious metal. This is usually a pure copper wire with a thin coating of silver; like color-coated wire, it's sometimes called craft wire. Some silver-plated wires have a nontarnish coating so they will stay bright and shiny. **Gold-plated** wire is made in the same way as silver-plated wire, but the copper wire is electroplated with a thin layer of gold. It's obviously much cheaper than solid gold wire, but it does have a tendency to tarnish fairly quickly.

TIP

Copper can turn some wearers' skin green; some people, due to their body chemistry, are more prone to this than others. If this happens, consider sealing your finished jewelry with clear lacquer spray.

A relative newcomer to the marketplace is **silver-filled** wire, which is similar to plated wire but has a much thicker bond of silver over the base metal. **Gold-filled** wire has a layer of at least 10-karat gold bonded to brass—that's about 100 times more gold than gold-plated wire. Gold-filled wire is durable and nontarnishing. Although it's a lot cheaper than solid gold, it is still quite expensive and is the wire of choice for those who want to create high-end gold wire jewelry.

Of course, the ultimate for most wireworkers is to be able to work in precious metals. **Sterling silver** is an alloy composed of 925/1000 parts pure silver and 75 parts pure copper. It is a dream to work with. It tarnishes due to the copper content, but it looks lovely when it's deliberately oxidized as well.

Fine silver is 99.99% pure silver and does not tarnish. It is soft and will never get as hard as sterling silver, which can be worked to hold its shape very well.

Few wireworkers use **solid gold** wire because of its high cost; gold-filled is an acceptable substitute. Solid gold is more malleable than gold-filled wire. Many other metals are suitable for the wireworker: Argentium sterling, niobium, platinum, palladium, steel, and aluminum, for example. When you have gained more experience, you may want to give them a try.

A variety of gauges in gold-filled and sterling silver wire.

Gauge

Gauge is the thickness of a wire. The American Wire Gauge (AWG) system uses number designations (the higher the number, the thinner the wire). You may also see wire measured in millimeters. The two systems don't align precisely, but they are close enough to be used interchangeably. I offer both measurements in this book and have rounded off the metric measurement for ease of use.

Choosing the correct gauge for a project is an important decision. For instance, if you are making earring wires, the wire must be thin enough to pass through the ear piercing but thick enough to hold its shape.

AWG	mm	BEST USED FOR
12	2.00	Bangles, cuffs
13	1.83	Cuff frames
14	1.63	Links, tiara bases
15	1.45	Tiara bands, chokers
16	1.29	Circlets, heavy clasps, frames
18	1.02	Simple loops, jump rings, links, clasps
20	0.81	Jump rings, earring wires, headpins, brooch pins
21	0.72	The perfect size for earring wires
22	0.64	Wrapped loops, headpins
24	0.51	Wire-wrapping, wrapped loops, coiling
26	0.40	Wire-wrapping, attaching frames together, coiling, weaving
28	0.32	Filigree work, wire-weaving, twisting
30	0.25	Crochet, knitting
32	0.23	Crochet, knitting

Use this chart as a handy reference to help you choose the correct gauge for your own designs. Thick gauges of wire (numbers less than 18/above 1mm) require practice and are not suitable for beginners. Only a few projects in this book require the use of 16 gauge/1.25mm wire. However, as soon as you feel up to the challenge, you should try them—particularly for chains, chokers, and clasps, which need to be sturdy.

Temper

This term refers to the resistance offered by the wire: how easy or difficult it is to bend and shape. Wire is tempered during manufacture and is identified on a scale of soft to spring-hard.

In handmade jewelry, we use only the soft end of the scale: **soft** (also called dead-soft) and **half-hard**. Wire that's harder than these tempers (such as memory wire) is very difficult to work with and will damage standard jewelry tools. When temper is not mentioned (in cheaper craft wires, for instance), count on it being at the soft end of the scale.

Don't worry too much about temper as you begin. Most wireworkers develop a preference for working with soft or half-hard wire as they gain more experience.

TEMPER	PROS AND CONS	BEST FOR
Soft or dead-soft	• Very malleable • Easy to bend and shape with fingers • Will lose its shape with little pressure • Easily marked • No springiness	• Wrapping other wires • Knitting and crochet • Wire-weaving • Making wrapped loops • When a lot of manipulation is necessary • Making small frames • Coiling • Making spirals
Half-hard	• Holds its shape well • Requires tools to work it • Springy • Harder on the hands	• Clasps and closures • Jump rings • Links and pins • Frames • Earring wires
Spring-hard Memory wire	• Holds its shape so well it does not require clasps • Durable • Will blunt ordinary jewelry tools • Extremely hard to work with	• Rigid bangles • Chokers • Rings

MATERIALS

Temper (continued)

Working with soft wire is easy on your hands, but the finished article will be quite malleable. What can you do to make the piece more durable and able to bear the stress of everyday wear? Try this: Take a small piece of soft wire in your fingers and bend it back and forth a few times. You will feel the wire becoming stiffer, and if you continue, it will eventually snap. This is called **work-hardening**.

Everything you do to your wire will harden it to some degree, such as running it through your fingers, polishing it with a cloth, bending it, hammering it, rubbing it against other wire or objects, burnishing it, and twisting it.

Conversely, you can make a hard wire soft by heating it to a certain temperature with a torch. This process is called **annealing**.

The goal in wireworking is to work-harden your wire so it becomes stiff enough to hold a desired shape but not so much that it becomes brittle and snaps. With practice, you'll become familiar with this ideal point.

Wire shape

Wire is manufactured by pulling rods of metal through increasingly smaller holes in steel plates until the desired gauge is reached. The shape of the holes determines the profile or shape of the wire.

Round wire is the most versatile and all-purpose shape, easily worked into curved components such as loops, spirals, and coils. Round wire is available in the widest number of gauges and is the shape used exclusively in this book.

Square wires fit neatly and securely against each other when stacked and bound together, and single square wires can be twisted for a decorative effect. Square is not the ideal shape for making loops or spirals.

Rectangular wire is useful for making wide ring bands. **Half-round** or D-shape wire can be used to make small, neat wraps, and thick gauges of half-round wire are used for making ring shanks.

Beads

Beautiful wirework enhances the beauty of beads and vice-versa, so we are not going to deny ourselves the pleasure of their company. There are so many millions to choose from; let your taste, your eyes, and your budget decide. There are, however, a few things to look out for when choosing beads to embellish wirework.

Bead measurements are universally expressed in millimeters (with the exception of seed beads). The size of the bead hole determines the gauge of the wire, so avoid large beads with tiny holes. Too large a hole can always be camouflaged, but too small a hole will inevitably lead to frustration. Freshwater pearls always have narrow drill holes, so make sure you take that into account.

A pet peeve of mine is to find a bead in which a narrow channel has been drilled from both sides but not aligned in the center. A flexible beading wire might make it through the hole, but rigid wire won't. Make a visual check for a clean passage through all gemstone beads before purchase.

Metal (wire) is stronger than glass. The vulnerable parts of glass or crystal beads are the edges of the hole, so discard any that are not in good condition.

Metal beads look very appealing in wirework jewelry. Bead caps and small, round metal beads are also very useful as protection for delicate beads. Buy seamless metal beads with large holes.

Findings

Findings got their name because they were made from the little scraps of metal that goldsmiths found on their workbenches at the end of the day. Findings link and hold together the various parts of your piece. In this book, you'll learn how to make your own findings so that your jewelry can be entirely handcrafted. However, to start, we will use a few commercial findings.

A **headpin** is simply wire with a stopper at one end that prevents a bead from falling off. Headpins are used to make dangles and drops. The stopper ranges from a simple flat head like a nail to more embellished and elaborate endings. Before we cut our first piece of wire from the spool, we'll create several projects using purchased 1½" (4cm) headpins as the starting point.

A **jump ring** is simply a ring cut from coiled wire. Using a jump ring is the simplest way to connect one part to another. The gauge and diameter of the ring are important considerations when choosing or making jump rings. Wirework made entirely of jump rings is called chain mail. This skillful interlocking of rings to achieve a supple yet impenetrable metal material was originally developed to make armor. For use in the projects, a size of 5–6mm (which refers to the outside diameter of the jump ring) is a good multipurpose size to keep on hand.

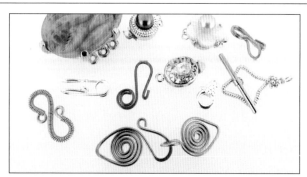

Clasps allow you to open and close your jewelry and are very important to the proper functioning of a piece. They add a decorative element and can even be made into the focal point.

 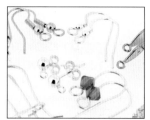

Bead caps, which fit neatly over the holes in beads, embellish and protect the beads.

Earring wires pass through a pierced earlobe. They have a loop so you can easily add to them to turn them into earrings. Most wireworkers make their own earring wires. You may want to purchase rubber or metal ear nuts (also called scrolls or backs) that are strung onto the wire to keep earrings secure.

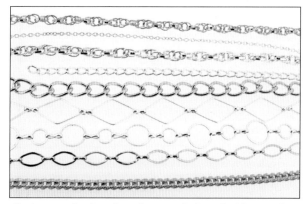

Chain is used to lengthen, decorate, link, and add strength and depth to a design.

You'll learn how to make many more types of findings as you work through this book.

TOOLS & WORKSPACE

To get started in wirework, you'll need only a few relatively inexpensive hand tools and very little in the way of specialized workspace. Acquiring a new set of tools is a pleasure, and it's amazing how attached you may become to your new helpers. Your most important tools are, of course, your hands—and because they are irreplaceable, you must always resist the temptation to use them instead of a tool (as you open a jump ring, for instance). You may want to choose ergonomic tools because you will be using them as an extension of your hands, sometimes for hours at a time. In wirework, we often use both hands equally. I'm told this is very good for keeping your brain young!

What to look for when choosing tools

Good-quality tools will last many years, produce better results, and are built to reduce stress in your hand muscles (not to mention your mental stress level!). The price is often a good indication of a tool's quality. If you are on a restricted budget, put most of your money into quality wire cutters and roundnose pliers.

You will find various sizes and types of handles available to suit your hands; tools that are designed to be especially ergonomic will be identified as such. Mini pliers can be handy if you are traveling, but they are uncomfortable to use over long periods. Longer handles give better leverage and reduce hand stress. Handles are made of metal, plastic rubber, or foam, and your choice will be largely a matter of preference and what feels most comfortable to you. Plastic rubber and foam have a cushioning effect. Foam gets dirty very quickly. Metal puts you in close touch with the wire.

A good tool feels well balanced, light, and comfortable in the hand. Run your fingers along the jaws; they should feel smooth with no nicks or burs on the metal. The pliers should open and close smoothly with no jerky action or undue resistance.

Absolutely essential

Pliers

The jaws of **roundnose pliers** look like two identical cones with pointed ends. These pliers are the tools you will use most for making loops, coils, and curved bends, so it's worth getting a quality pair. When the jaws are closed, you should see a tiny, tapering gap between the jaws. The tips should be perfectly aligned. You can complete all the projects in this book with a single mid-size pair.

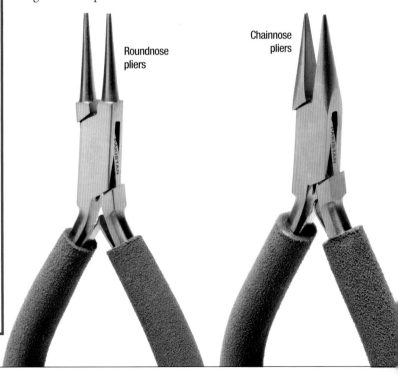

Roundnose pliers

Chainnose pliers

Chainnose pliers look like two half cones tapering to a point on the outside. The insides of the jaws are smooth. The tiny, sharp tips are very useful for getting into tight spots. Chainnose pliers are used to open and close jump rings and loops, hold small parts securely, and flatten wire ends.

Bentnose pliers are very similar in function to chainnose pliers but the tips of the jaws are bent upward. These bent tips are very useful for getting into awkward places. The angle of the nose reduces wrist stress. Because you need two pairs of pliers to open jump rings, I suggest you buy one pair of chainnose and one pair of bentnose.

The jaws of **flatnose pliers** are flat on all sides, and the jaw tips are wide. They are used for flattening wire, making spirals, and making sharp angles. Anytime you want to make a crisp right angle (and I love those!), this is the tool to use.

Wire cutters

When choosing your wire cutters, look for:

- **A clean, quick, one-action cut.**
- **Side-cutting jaws with sharp points.**
- **Maximum gauge recommendation.** All good cutters have this information. It's the maximum wire size and metal (usually copper) that you can cut without causing damage to your pliers. Look for a cutter that cuts no less than 16-gauge (1.25mm) copper. For thicker gauges, use a household or memory-wire cutter. Even one trim of a thicker gauge than recommended will ruin your pliers.

Cutters compress the wire from both sides when cutting, so a little metal peak is left in the center. This is called a **beveled cut**. All cutters will do this to some extent, but some cutters leave **flush** ends. You'll see these called "flush cutters" or "ultra-flush cutters." Because you'll usually file the ends of wires, this is desirable but need not be your most important consideration.

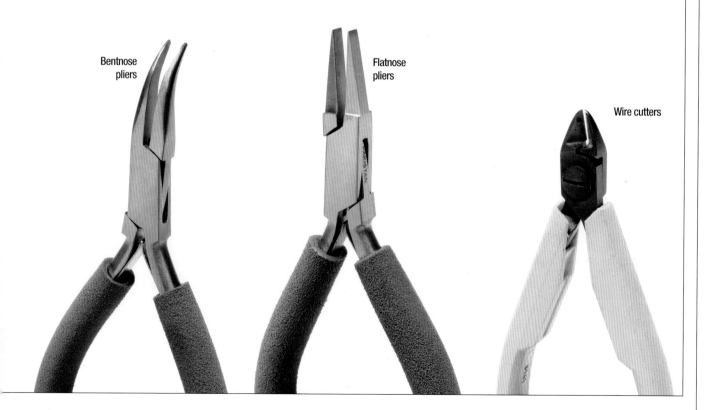

Bentnose pliers

Flatnose pliers

Wire cutters

TOOLS & WORKSPACE

Hammers

There are dozens of hammer types available, but only two are absolutely essential as you begin. A **chasing hammer** has a flat face for flattening wire and a rounded face for forming a gentle curve. A **nylon-head mallet** or **rawhide mallet** can be used to work-harden your wire without flattening it. Nylon heads are replaceable.

Bench block or anvil

You need a hard, smooth, tempered steel surface on which to place your work for hammering. You can purchase a bench block or anvil. To economize, use the side of a large, polished hammer.

Files

These are used to smooth away burs (scratchy bits) made by other tools. Specialized jewelry files are called **needle files**. They come in various shapes to get into tight corners but can be fairly expensive. To begin with, emery, metal, or diamond **nail files** will do the job adequately; buy a range of grits.

Mandrels

A mandrel is any hard object, usually cylindrical, that you can use to shape wire. You have lots of those around the house already: knitting needles, pens, cans, vases, empty bobbins, pipes, bead tubes…the list is endless. I use an old wooden pencil to form my earring wires. For a long time before I purchased a proper bracelet mandrel, I used a small can of peas. If you plan to make rings, I recommend using a ring mandrel, which really helps in sizing. Otherwise, look around the house for objects in handy sizes.

Other essential supplies

A **bead mat** made of soft, nappy Vellux is inexpensive and invaluable. It protects your work surface, anchors your work, stops beads from running away, and safely gathers bits of wire. You'll also need:
- **pencil and paper** for making notes
- a **permanent marker**
- a **ruler** (preferably metal)
- a **measuring tape**
- a large **jewelry-polishing cloth**

These essential supplies are not listed in each project's supply list, so always have them on hand.

Left to right: rawhide mallet, utility hammer, chasing hammer, nylon-head mallet.

Left to right: flat file, needle file, diamond nail file, and emery boards.

A variety of mandrels, including household items.

Left to right: pencil and paper, a permanent marker, measuring tape, metal ruler, and a polishing cloth—all on a bead mat.

TIP Cut your polishing cloth into small pieces and it will last a lot longer.

Optional tools

As you acquire skills and venture into challenging projects, you may feel the need for some additional helpers. Consider these optional tools as you progress:

Parallel-jaw pliers give you a fantastic grip without marking the wire. The gap between the jaws remains the same as you squeeze the handle. They are ideal for twisting several wires together and forming spirals. The downside is that they are heavy and a bit awkward to use.

A crimping tool, made for working with flexible beading wire, is useful for pressing the wire ends of wrapped loops enatly against the neck of the loop. A **wire rounder** (also called a **cup bur**) has a tiny cup with teeth inside that smooth the tips of wire for earrings. **Nylon-jaw pliers** have replaceable jaws that can straighten wire, hold loops, and form spirals without marring the wire.

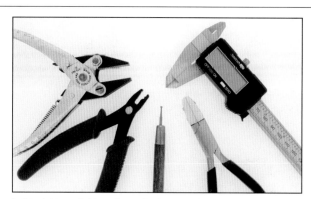

Left to right: parallel-jaw pliers, crimping tool, wire rounder, nylon-jaw pliers, and digital calipers.

Placing a piece of polishing cloth inside the jaws of standard flatnose pliers does the job as well.

Digital calipers give accurate measurements of wire thickness and bead sizes.

Workspace

Wirework does not require a huge amount of space, so you can easily get set up whether you have your own studio, steal space from other rooms in the house, or even prefer to work in front of the TV.

Make sure you have good lighting and sit in a comfortable chair with good lumbar support. Try to keep clutter to a minimum (although I have to admit that I don't always succeed with this point!).

Choose your bead colors in daylight, even if you do your wirework at night. You will avoid some unpleasant surprises.

Storage

Store your wire in plastic bags and boxes with anti-tarnish strips or pieces of chalk to prevent tarnishing.

Keep sterling silver labeled and separate from other types of wire; narrow gauges are particularly difficult to identify if mixed up. Scrap sterling can also be sold to metal reclaimers.

Care of your tools

- Very thick gauges or hard wire will damage your tools—especially cutters and roundnose pliers. Use tools made for household use when working with heavy wire.
- Store your pliers upright so the tips don't get damaged and they don't scratch each other. Empty large food cans (washed and thoroughly dried, of course!) make ideal containers to hook tool handles on.
- Never immerse your tools in water. Use a damp cloth to clean the handles if necessary and dry thoroughly.
- File and sand nicks, scratches, and burs on your tools as you find them.
- Occasionally put a small dab of oil on the pliers' joints.
- Files become clogged up and inefficient very quickly. Regularly tap out wire filings and clean the joints with an old, dry toothbrush.

Have everything you need?
On to the projects!

Projects

HOW TO

measure wire using guide beads • form a perfectly round simple loop
• open and close a loop • safely hammer a loop • size a bracelet

PROJECT 1
Chunky charm bracelet

Forming a simple loop is a key skill that you'll learn first. Wire loops secure beads and connect beads to each other or to other findings. In this project , you'll string beads on headpins—short pieces of wire that have a stopper on one end. I'll also introduce a neat trick that will save time and help you achieve consistent and accurate results: using a guide bead (GB for short).

Perfectly round, even loops are a sign of good workmanship. Soon you'll be making beautiful loops almost automatically.

Length: 7–8"(18–20cm)

WHAT YOU'LL NEED

- **25** (29) headpins
- Readymade medium-link curb chain with clasp
- **12** (13) 12mm round beads
- **6** (7) 10mm diamond-shape beads
- **6** (7) 10–12mm assorted metal charms
- **6** bead caps (optional)
- Wire cutters
- Chainnose or bentnose pliers
- Flatnose pliers
- Roundnose pliers
- Bench block or anvil
- Chasing hammer
- Scrap of card stock or thin plastic
- 10mm guide bead (GB)

Sizing

Measure your wrist with a measuring tape just below the protruding bone and add 1" (2.5cm) to find your size. The quantities listed first are for a 7" (18cm) bracelet. Use the quantities in parentheses to make an 8" (20cm) bracelet.

Safety first

Wire cutters release a huge amount of energy, and a cut wire end can fly off with great force. This can be very dangerous—not just for yourself but for other people or pets in the same room. Always either place your index finger over the piece being cut or direct it downward. Burying the tip in the bead mat before you cut is very safe and makes it easy to gather the cut ends.

1. String a bead cap, a bead, and a 10mm guide bead (GB) on a headpin.

2. Press the head of the headpin against your finger and bury the end in the bead mat. Place the slightly opened jaws of the cutters with the flat side next to the GB. Slide the beads tight against the head of the headpin.

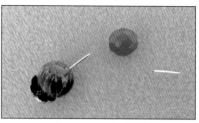

3. Squeeze the jaws firmly to cut the wire. Remove the GB. Your headpin is now cut to the correct size. If you use the same GB throughout the piece, all your loops will be consistent in size.

4. Here's a good way to hold the bead so it doesn't slip (it's a bit like holding a syringe): Press the head of the headpin with your thumb and push down on the bead on either side of the headpin with your index and middle fingers.

5. Hold the bead firmly and press the index finger of your other hand down on the wire close to the bead hole until the wire is at a right angle to the bead. Your dominant thumb will act as an anchor on the bead. The bead is now held securely in the headpin.

6. Keep holding the bead in your nondominant hand and continue: Grasp the tip of the wire firmly with roundnose pliers, working about halfway down the jaws. Make sure that the wire does not protrude beyond the jaws (this would make the loop oval in shape) and that it stays at a right angle to the pliers.

7. Begin slowly rotating the pliers clockwise while applying continuous downward pressure.

8. Continue rotating the pliers. Rotate slowly and firmly without letting go of the pliers. (It's a little like locking a door with a key.) Rotate as far as you can go.

9. You have now formed a nice, round loop, but it is still partly open.

Using guide beads (GBs)

Here are three ordinary beads of varying sizes. Cheap plastic or metal beads with large holes are ideal. Choose the guide bead (we'll call them GB for short) size to match the wire gauge: the thicker the gauge, the longer the GB. These GBs are 10mm, 12mm, and 14mm. These are the sizes I call for throughout this book, but you can choose other sizes to guide the sizes of the loops you make.

10. Now you'll make a series of small movements designed to close the loop while retaining its round shape. It's like rolling out pastry: You can't roll it all in one move; you have to do it in small, repeated motions. First, reposition the neck of the loop backwards: With the tip of the roundnose pliers, push down on the part of the wire closest to the bead. Some wireworkers call this "breaking the neck."

11. The neck of the loop is now broken, but the loop is still round and holds the bead firmly in place. This move ensures that the loop stays centered.

12. Position the roundnose pliers so a little wire shows. The jaw must not fill the loop as it did before; leave some space between the wire and the pliers. Close the jaws and rotate the pliers slightly to push the wire into place to close the gap in the loop.

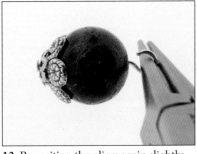

13. Reposition the pliers again slightly farther back on the loop and push the end of the wire to close the loop.

14. It may take a few more moves of the pliers to close a loop depending on the size of the loop and the thickness of the wire. However, the principle is the same: Take your time and make tiny movements. Steps 12 and 13 will ensure that the bead is firmly held between the end of the headpin and the loop.

15. Make ¹⁄₁₆ x ¼" (2 x 6mm) notch in a piece of stiff card or plastic. So that the loop does not lose its shape and pull open, it must be work-hardened. It's a tiny area to hammer and you risk hitting the bead or your fingers. The notch in the card will help you hammer the loop in a safe and easy way. We'll call this our **guard**. Keep it handy and use it every time you make simple loops.

Choose the right hammer for the job

Striking with any type of hammer will work-harden wire to some degree. Use the flat face of the **chasing hammer** for flattening wire and use the rounded end for texturing the metal. Use a **nylon-head** or **rawhide mallet** when you want the wire to keep its shape. Metal hammers work-harden wire fairly quickly; you will need to hammer for a much longer time with nylon or rawhide to work-harden the wire.

TIP

Pin both ends of the chain to your bead mat to keep it flat and make it easier to attach the beads.

16. Slide the notch of the guard between the bead and the loop and place the loop on the bench block. Hold the bead in place, keeping a finger on the headpin. Gently hammer the loop several times.

17. Open the loop by grasping the wire end with flatnose pliers and twisting the wire sideways. Do not pull the end toward you.

18. Make a total of six bead units with bead caps, six (seven) without bead caps, seven (eight) with diamond beads, and six (seven) with metal charms.

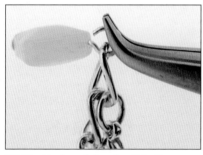

19. To attach each bead unit to the chain, open the loop and string it on a link. Close the loop by twisting in reverse. You will not be able to do this in one move; wriggle the end of the wire back and forth past the closing point while pushing on it firmly until the gap in the loop is completely closed. Wire is naturally springy and you have to allow for a small recoil to get it into position. Attach one bead unit per link.

Well done! You can now show off your very first wirework project.

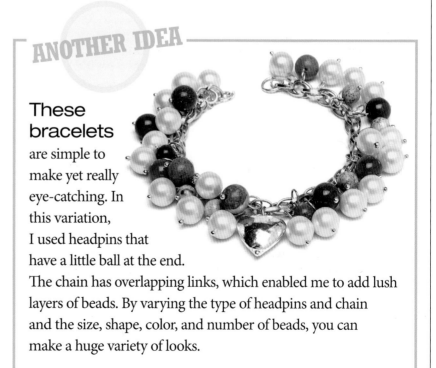

ANOTHER IDEA

These bracelets

are simple to make yet really eye-catching. In this variation, I used headpins that have a little ball at the end. The chain has overlapping links, which enabled me to add lush layers of beads. By varying the type of headpins and chain and the size, shape, color, and number of beads, you can make a huge variety of looks.

PROJECT2
Spinning top earrings

Let's practice what you learned in the first project by making these quick, easy, and perfectly formed earrings.

Length: 2" (5cm)

WHAT YOU'LL NEED

- **2** headpins
- **2** 10mm focal beads
- **4** 3mm metal beads
- **4** 2mm metal or seed beads (optional)
- **4** bead caps
- **2** jump rings
- Pair of earring wires
- Wire cutters
- Bentnose pliers
- Flatnose pliers
- Roundnose pliers
- 10mm GB

TIP

Many times a bead that's somewhat flattened does not sit well between bead caps. To fix this, place one or more small metal or seed beads between the bead and the cap. No more wobbles!

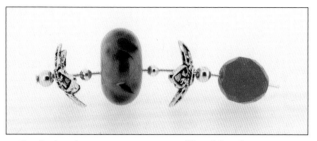

1. On the headpin, string: 3mm metal bead, bead cap, 2mm bead, 10mm focal bead, 2mm bead, bead cap, 3mm metal bead, GB.

2. Slide the beads to the end of the pin and trim the wire next to the GB.

3. Press the wire down at a right angle over the metal bead. Use roundnose pliers to make a loop.

4. Use flatnose pliers in a wriggling motion to close any gap and ensure that the end of the loop is firmly wedged above the bead.

5. To open a jump ring, use two pairs of pliers: Bring one end of the ring toward you at the same time you push the other away.

6. Slide the loop you made and the loop of the earring wire onto the jump ring. Use pliers to close the jump ring, reversing the motion you made in step 5. As you close the ring, add some pressure to push the ends toward each other. Move the ends slightly past the point of closure and back again until the ends align perfectly and you see no gap. Make a second earring.

ANOTHER IDEA

With these simple wirework skills, you can create a whole wardrobe of earrings! Use short lengths of chain or attach beads to chain links for new looks.

PROJECT 3
Drop earrings

Drop earrings are a classic type of earrings consisting of a bead link and a bead drop. A bead link consists of a bead that is sandwiched firmly between two simple loops that can be opened easily to connect other jewelry components. In this project, the bead link connects the earring wire and the drop bead.

Length: 2⅜" (6cm)

WHAT YOU'LL NEED

- Spool of 20-gauge (0.8mm) wire; you will use about 3" (8cm)
- **2** headpins
- **2** 6–10mm focal beads
- **2** drop beads with vertical holes
- **8** 2–3mm daisy metal spacers
- **8** 2–3mm flat spacer beads
- Wire cutters
- Bentnose pliers
- Flatnose pliers
- Bench block with guard
- **2** 10mm GBs

Working off the wire spool

Working off the spool simply means that you work on the end of the wire while it's still attached to the coil or spool instead of cutting a length first.

Advantages:
- you don't have to measure first, so you'll never run out of wire
- less waste because you only use what you need
- you have a longer piece to work with

Disadvantages:
- you must remember to string the beads first
- requires planning, because bead sequences cannot be changed
- can be a bit awkward to handle

1. On the end of the wire, string: GB, flat spacer, daisy spacer, focal bead, daisy spacer, flat spacer, GB.

2. Slide the last GB strung to the end of the wire and use your index finger to be sure you can feel the end of the wire. Place the flatnose pliers next to the GB.

3. Remove the GB and bend the wire at a right angle against the pliers.

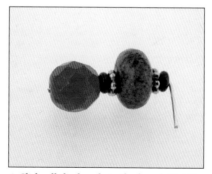

4. Slide all the beads to the bend. Cut the wire close to the GB.

5. Remove the second GB and bend the wire in the opposite direction.

TIP A combination of first working off the spool by stringing the bead sequence and then estimating and cutting the wire would also save a lot of waste.

6. Make a loop at each end to make a bead connector unit. Gently hammer the loops to work-harden them.

7. On a headpin, string: flat spacer, daisy spacer, drop bead, daisy spacer, flat spacer, and GB. Use wire cutters to push all the beads to the head of the headpin. Bury the wire end in the bead mat and trim next to the GB. Make a loop.

8. Open the loop on the drop by twisting it sideways with bentnose pliers. Slide the bead connector unit on and close the loop by twisting back.

9. Open the earring wire loop by twisting it sideways with bentnose pliers. Close the loop. Make a second earring.

ANOTHER IDEA

You can now make a wide selection of long, dangly earrings using a variety of beads in clusters or alone.

PROJECT4

Cleopatra's circlet

For the fourth project, your goal is a stunning piece that will give you practice in making loops and advance your skills at the same time. Make sure the rondelles and bead caps fit comfortably on the wire before you start.

Length: 15" (38cm)

WHAT YOU'LL NEED

- 8" (20cm) 16-gauge (1.25mm) wire
- 8–9" (20–23cm) chain
- **15** headpins
- **15** 10mm diamond-shaped flat beads
- **16** 6 x 8mm large-hole faceted rondelles
- **15** 2mm metal beads
- **32** small bead caps
- **2** jump rings
- **2** lobster claw clasps
- Wire cutters
- Bentnose pliers
- Chainnose pliers
- Roundnose pliers
- Bench block with guard
- Chasing hammer
- 10mm and 14mm GBs

1. On a headpin, string a 2mm metal bead, a diamond-shaped bead, and a 10mm GB. Flush-cut the wire.

2. Remove the GB and bend the wire at a right angle over the bead.

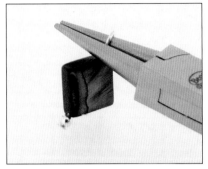

3. Using roundnose pliers, make a loop as we have learned. Prepare a total of 15 dangles in this way.

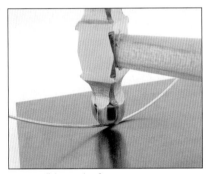

4. Cut 8" (20cm) of 16-gauge (1.25mm) wire. Place the centerpoint of the wire on the bench block. Hammer gently from the center outward to the ends with the ball part of the hammer until you have a semicircle. This should be done just once with gentle tapping; don't flatten the wire at all.

5. Measure the end with a 14mm GB. Place flatnose pliers next to the GB.

6. Remove the GB, bend the wire at a right angle, and make a loop as before.

TIP Gather a number of beads together on a bead mat. Unusual and pleasing combinations sometimes occur by chance. String beads on a spare piece of wire to give you an idea of what the finished piece will look like.

7. On the wire, string a pattern of bead cap, rondelle, bead cap, and dangle 15 times. String a bead cap, a rondelle, and a bead cap.

8. Slide all the beads to the loop, checking that you see no gaps. Place flatnose pliers against the last bead cap and bend the wire at a right angle.

9. Place a 14mm GB on the wire and flush-cut. Make a loop.

10. Use a guard to hammer the two loops flat. The loops will now be slightly open. Close them tightly by wriggling the ends back and forth with the flatnose pliers.

11. Cut an 8–9" (21–23cm) piece of chain. Open a jump ring and attach a clasp to both ends of the chain.

Try out the rondelle beads and bead caps on the wire before you start. They should fit comfortably to allow for slight expansion of the wire after hammering. Use 18-gauge (1mm) wire if in doubt.

12. Clip the chain to both ends of the circlet.

ANOTHER IDEA

Make a stunning

matching bracelet using three small circlet sections made of 2¾" (7cm) pieces of 18-gauge (1mm) wire. Link the sections with two jump rings each and hang some metal charms for extra fun. Or attach chain as you did for the necklace to make a choker.

PROJECT 5
Big bead splash

Length: 29" (74cm)

WHAT YOU'LL NEED

- 45" (115cm) 22-gauge (0.6mm) half-hard wire
- **9** 25mm round coin beads (jasper)
- **9** 12mm beads (lava)
- **18** 8mm gemstone beads (carnelian)
- **18** 3mm metal beads
- **18** 2–3mm daisy spacers
- Wire cutters
- Bentnose pliers
- Chainnose pliers
- Flatnose pliers
- Roundnose pliers

This design requires no clasp because it's long enough to go over your head. Under the weight of the big, delicious turquoise beads, a simple loop would most likely open, so we'll learn how to make a secure wrapped loop. Wrapped loops lend a different look to your designs and require a bit more planning.

TIP

Remembering to link a component before doing the second wrap can be a problem. So many times I have concentrated all my attention on making a beautifully wrapped looped only to discover that it was too late to link it. I now write LINK FIRST on a bright sticky note in front of me. It helps, although it's not foolproof!

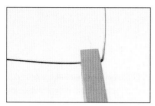

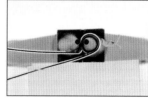

1. Cut a 5" (13cm) length of wire. Mark a 2" (5cm) tail, grasp next to the mark with flatnose pliers, and bend the wire in a sharp right angle with your fingers.

2. Mark the roundnose pliers using one of the methods suggested below. Place the bend in the wire between the jaws of the roundnose pliers on the mark you have made.

3. With your fingers, push the wire tail over and around the marked jaw.

4. Keeping the wire in place, rotate the pliers clockwise (as though you're unlocking a door) and press the wire tail against the jaw. The loop will look somewhat like an old-fashioned keyhole.

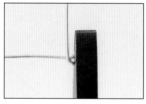

5. Remove the roundnose pliers from the loop and grasp the whole loop with flatnose pliers. Use your thumb to bend the wire tail into a right angle.

6. Keep holding the whole loop firmly in the pliers while wrapping the wire around the stem. The best way to do this is to push it with the side of your thumb as far as it will go, making sure the wire remains at a right angle.

7. With the wire toward the back of the loop, use the side of your index finger to wrap until you can take over with your thumb again. This close and constant contact with the wire gives you excellent control over the tightness and positioning of the wraps.

8. After you've made three close wraps, flush-cut the wrapping wire close to the wraps, angling the cutters to create a slight wedge shape. Use the tip of bentnose pliers to flatten the end and tuck it neatly next to the wraps.

 TIP Wrap very slowly while applying steady pressure on the wire for a neat, even look.

 TIP Cutting the wire end in a wedge shape makes it easier to flatten against the neck and gives a smoother appearance.

How to make same-size loops every time

For a professional look, make all of your loops the same size. One way to achieve this is to mark the exact spot where you make the loops on the jaw of the roundnose pliers. Here are a few suggestions; try them and soon you'll find your favorite.

1. Simply mark the jaw of your roundnose pliers with a permanent marker. You may need to remark the spot every so often.

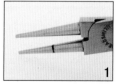

2. Wrap the jaw with tape and use the edge of the tape as a mark. Or mark right on the tape: This adds a layer of cushion to the jaws.

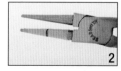

3. Wrap a piece of very thin wire around the jaw and secure it with a few twists. Keep it on the jaw and make loops just above it. This technique does not mark the pliers, enables you to make different sizes in one jewelry piece, and can be kept handy to make the same size of loops later. This can be a little awkward to use at first. I use a different color of craft wire to signify each of my favorite loop sizes.

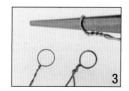

9. String an 8mm bead, a daisy spacer, a donut bead, a daisy spacer, and an 8mm bead and push them firmly against the wraps. Place the tip of the bentnose pliers against the last bead and bend the wire over the pliers at a right angle.

10. Repeat steps 2–5. You should have one closed wrapped loop and one open unfinished loop ready to be strung onto another component. Make a total of nine more three-bead components.

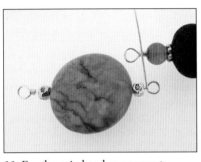

11. For the coin bead components, repeat steps 1–10, replacing the stringing sequence of step 9 with this pattern: 3mm metal bead, 25mm coin bead, 3mm metal bead. Make a total of nine coin bead components.

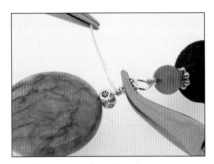

12. Alternating three-bead components with coin bead components, string the open loop of one piece through the closed loop of another. Hold the loop firmly with the tip of bentnose pliers and repeat steps 6–8 to close.

ANOTHER IDEA

Give a dainty look to earrings by using very thin wire for the wrapped loops. Crystals and wire thicker than 24-gauge (0.4mm) don't mix very well because crystals chip easily. Instead of making a thicker gauge simple loop and risking breakage, make a pretty wrapped loop with thinner wire and the crystal will be perfectly safe and secure.

Which loop to choose?

Use simple loops:
- with commercial headpins, which tend to be stiff and difficult to wrap
- with thick gauges (typically, thicker than 21-gauge (0.7mm))
- in designs where loops are put under minimal stress (for example, in earring dangles)
- with hard wire

Use wrapped loops:
- with thin gauges (finer than 22-gauge (0.6mm))
- in designs where the loop is under stress and risks opening
- with small-hole beads

TIP

When using a really springy wire or to complete a final wrap, use the tip of the chainnose pliers to pull the wire around.

PROJECT6
Sweet spiral earrings

Spirals and scrolls are an ancient form of decoration found in everyday objects, art, and architecture throughout the ages. These shapes and their endless variations have never lost their appeal.

In wirework, spirals are a practical way of finishing wire ends and connecting parts of jewelry. The shape of the spiral is determined by the first coil you make, so the start of the spiral is very important. Speed is the enemy of well-made spirals. Every movement you make should be tiny and slow.

Length: 3" (8cm)

WHAT YOU'LL NEED

- 36" (92cm) 20-gauge (0.8mm) soft wire
- **2** 8mm focal beads
- **10** 3mm metal beads
- **10** 2mm saucer beads
- Pair of earring wires
- Wire cutters
- Bentnose pliers
- Flatnose pliers
- Roundnose pliers
- Bench block and guard
- Chasing hammer
- Guard
- File
- 10mm and 14mm GBs

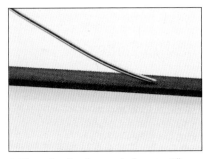

1. To make the short spirals, cut a 2" (5cm) piece of wire, trimming one end in a wedge shape. Place the file on your work surface and rub the wire end on the file in one direction only (away from you).

2. With tip of the roundnose pliers, grasp the wedge end of the wire just below the wedge and form a tiny loop. You are basically tucking the thin end of the wire inside the loop.

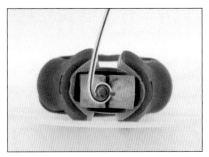

3. Reposition the pliers and form the wire halfway around the top of the first loop as shown. This will create enough of a spiral to grasp in the next step.

4. Grasp the whole loop very firmly in chainnose or bentnose pliers as shown, with just a little of the spiral showing. Position the middle of your thumb on the straight part of the wire and push it against the spiral for a quarter turn. Reposition the pliers to grasp the new part of the spiral. Continue in the same way until you have made three spirals.

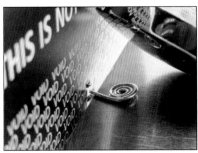

5. Place the spiral on the bench block. Hold it with the guard and hammer it flat.

6. Place the 10mm GB on the tail and flush-cut the wire.

7. Place flatnose pliers below the straight wire tail and bend the wire at a right angle over the pliers and perpendicular to the plane of the spiral.

8. Make a loop. Make a second, mirror-image spiral component.

TIP

Cutting the end of the wire in a wedge shape and filing it avoids a bump in the first spiral. The thicker the gauge, the more pronounced the bump. This technique is useful for making perfectly round loops.

9. To make the medium-length spirals, cut 2½" (6.5cm) of wire and follow steps 1–5. String a saucer bead, a metal bead, and a 10mm GB. Slide the GB to the top of the wire, place flatnose pliers below it, remove the GB, and bend the wire at a right angle, perpendicular to the spiral. Make a loop. Make a second, mirror-image medium-length spiral.

10. To make the long spiral, cut 3" (7.5cm) of wire and proceed as for the medium spirals, but make only one. To center the wire over the spiral, place the tip of the flatnose pliers above the spiral and break the neck.

ANOTHER IDEA

11. Cut 3" (7.5cm) of wire. Place a 14mm GB on the end and the flatnose pliers under the bead. Bend the wire at a right angle and make a loop. Hammer the loop lightly and then open it. Making sure that the side spirals are facing out, string a small spiral, a medium spiral, a long spiral, a medium spiral, and a short spiral on the loop.

12. On the straight wire end, string a 3mm metal bead, a saucer bead, a focal bead, a saucer bead, a metal bead, and a 10mm GB. Trim the wire, remove the GB, and make a loop. Hammer flat using the guard. Attach an earring wire. Make a second earring.

Pick out colors

in a focal bead and make a tassel of matching beads on spiraled headpins strung on lengths of chain.

PROJECT 7
Spiral pendant choker

Length: 16½" (42cm)

WHAT YOU'LL NEED

- 26" (66cm) 16-gauge (1.25mm) soft wire
- 20 x 30mm rectangle bead
- Wire cutters
- Bentnose pliers
- Flatnose pliers
- Roundnose pliers
- Bench block
- Chasing hammer
- File
- **2** 14mm GBs

Open spirals are essentially free-form, so you really can do no wrong. Using soft wire will give you the best results; you can harden it after you shape it. This simple but elegant design showcases a single large bead. You could also hang a matching drop at the bottom of the spiral. The gauge given for the choker is the minimum you should use; the bead loops and spiral can be made with finer gauges if you like. For a good fit, measure the base of your neck and add 4" (10cm).

1. Flush-cut 6" (15cm) of wire. Mark the center and file the ends smooth. With roundnose pliers, make a half loop with one turn of your wrist. Spiral the wire loosely using your fingers.

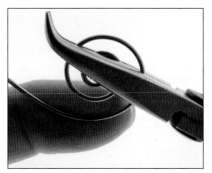

2. After the second turn, hold the spiral with bentnose pliers. For an even gap between the coils, push your index finger pad between the coils while pushing the wire end with your thumb. You should feel the center of your finger pad being lightly pinched between the wires.

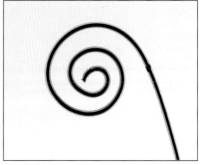

3. Continue in this way, making small movements and repositioning the pliers frequently until you reach the center mark.

4. Make a mirror-image spiral on the other end of the wire. Fix any inequalities using your fingers. When you are satisfied with the shape, hammer it flat on the bench block.

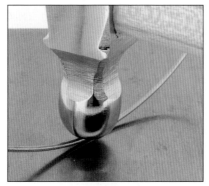

5. To make the choker wire, cut 17" (43cm) of wire or use your neck measurement plus 4" (10cm). Working with the natural curve of the wire straight off the spool, place the center of the U shape on the block and hammer gently from the center to the ends with the ball part of the hammer.

6. Place the GB on one end of the wire and grasp the wire with flatnose pliers directly below the bead.

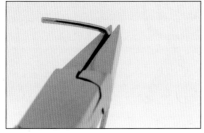

7. Remove the GB and bend the end of the wire toward the inside of the curve at a right angle.

TIP The motion of forming an open spiral is similar to winding a soft measuring tape. Using your fingers instead of tools will ensure much better control of coiling and avoid dents and bumps caused by tools. It's good fun and it will help you to get to know your wire.

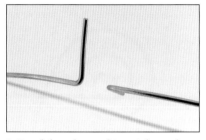

8. Bend the other end in a right angle that is perpendicular to the plane of the curve.

9. Make a slightly open loop on each end. The ends simply hook into each other and remain closed due to tension. Unhook the ends several times and gently stretch the curve until the wire has the correct amount of tension.

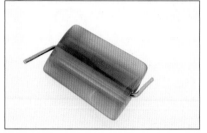

10. Place the focal bead on a wire from the spool and use two 14mm GBs to measure and trim the wire. Make mirror-image loops at each end.

11. Attach one loop to the spiral and the other to the choker.

ANOTHER IDEA

This is a much more elaborate choker. Make sure you string the beads before making the closure loop. To keep the beads from escaping through the closure, hammer flat a small area of the wire on both sides. If you are adding drop beads, close the loops on the spiral so the drops don't slip out.

PROJECT8
In the pink bracelet

Simply by increasing the inside diameter of a wire spiral, you can turn it into a strong and pretty connector. In this bracelet, a single dangle sits in the center of the double spiral. If you like a really jangly bracelet, you can hang small dangles on either side as well.

Length: 8¼" (21cm)

WHAT YOU'LL NEED

- 65" (165cm) 18-gauge (1mm) soft wire
- **6** 12mm focal beads
- **6** 6 x 8mm rondelle beads
- **24** bead caps
- Wire cutters
- Bentnose pliers
- Flatnose pliers
- Roundnose pliers
- Bench block and guard
- Chasing hammer
- 12mm GB

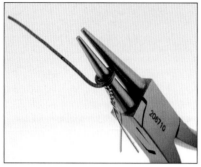

1. To make the connectors, mark the roundnose pliers in your chosen way halfway down the jaw. Cut 2½" (6.5cm) of wire and mark the centerpoint. Grasp the end of the wire, making sure it does not protrude from the jaws, and make a loop. Rotate the pliers to start a second loop around the first.

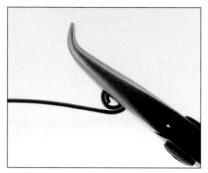

2. Place the loops in the bentnose pliers and push the wire against the spiral until you reach the mark.

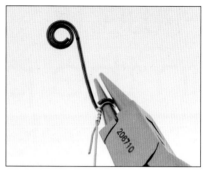

3. Repeat step 1, this time forming the loop in the opposite direction.

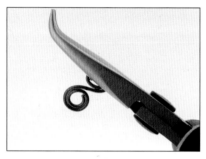

4. Repeat step 2 until you see only a small gap between the spirals. Hammer the spirals flat. Make a total of six spiral connectors.

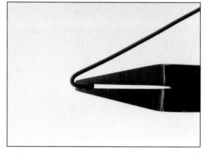

5. To make the oval spiral, flush-cut 5½" (14cm) of wire. Place the last ⅛" (3mm) inside the tip of flatnose pliers as shown. Hold the pliers firmly and bend the wire over the tip of the jaw in a tight U shape.

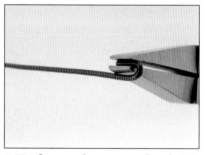

6. Use flatnose pliers to complete the U shape as shown. Grasp the entire shape and flatten it. Start from the bend and work slowly.

7. Hold the flattened bend with flatnose pliers while pushing the wire with your thumb to make the spiral. Reposition the pliers after each bend.

8. Rotate four times, ending with the wire at the top. Hammer the spiral flat, avoiding the wire tail. Place the flatnose pliers as shown and make a right-angle bend directly above the center of the spiral. The straight end of the wire will be centered over the spiral.

9. String a bead cap, a rondelle bead, a bead cap, and a GB. Flush-cut the wire. Make a loop and hammer flat using the guard. Make a total of six dangles.

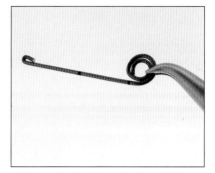

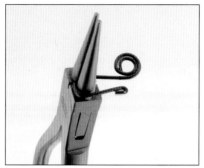

10. To make the clasp, flush-cut 2½" (6.5cm) of wire. Mark the centerpoint and make another mark ½" (13mm) from the first. Repeat steps 1 and 2 to form a spiral up to the center mark. Bend the other end as in steps 5 and 6.

11. Place the wire at the base of the roundnose pliers with the second mark positioned as shown. Bend the wire around the base of the jaw and toward the spiral into a hook shape. Use the flat face of the chasing hammer to strike the curved part of the hook until it is flat.

ANOTHER IDEA

Make a lovely
pair of matching earrings using an earring wire, a connector, and a dangle.

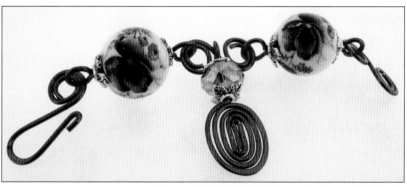

12. Working off the wire spool, string a GB, a bead cap, a focal bead, a bead cap, and a GB. Make loops on both sides of the bead and hammer them lightly to work-harden them. Make a total of six focal-bead links. To assemble the bracelet, alternate bead links and connectors. Attach the hook clasp to one end and attach the dangles on the gap between the spirals.

TIP

To avoid chipping the coating of colored wire, you can place a piece of cardboard on the piece before hammering it flat.

Cleaning and straightening wire prior to use

Wire thicker than 22-gauge (0.6mm) should always be cleaned before use. You also may need to smooth out kinks and straighten the curve it retains from the spool.
Cleaning: Some metals tarnish, no matter how carefully they are stored, and a finished piece of wirework jewelry can be very difficult to polish once assembled. Sandwich the wire inside a piece of polishing cloth. Run the cloth the whole length of the wire, squeezing it tightly between your fingers. Repeat several times.
Straightening: Leaving the wire on the spool for anchorage, grip the wire in nylon-jaw pliers and run

along to the end. If you've already cut the wire, grip one end firmly in chainnose pliers while you run it through the nylon-jaw pliers. You may have to do this several times; each time, the wire will stiffen a little more. Wires from different manufacturers harden at a different rate, so you need to experiment.

You can also clean and straighten at the same time by placing a piece of jewelry cloth inside the jaws of nylon-jaw or flatnose pliers and running it along the length of the wire.

PROJECT 9

Spiral sizzle neckpiece

As you work on this challenging project, you'll learn how to shape many variations on the spiral theme. You'll make all of the components first and then link them. You do not have to stick rigidly to the suggested type or size of beads, but make sure all the bead holes are large enough before you begin. Start from the center and add as many or as few of the side dangles as you like. The design possibilities are limitless.

Length: 16½" (42cm)

WHAT YOU'LL NEED

- 11¼' (3.50m) of 18-gauge (1mm) soft wire
- Set of 5 coin beads (18mm, **2** 15mm, **2** 12mm)
- **26** 6 x 8mm rondelle beads
- Wire cutters
- Bentnose pliers
- Flatnose pliers
- Roundnose pliers
- Bench block and guard
- Chasing hammer
- **2** 12mm GBs

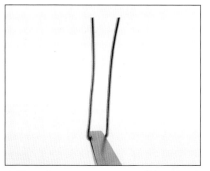

1. To make a connector, cut 3" (8cm) of wire and mark the centerpoint. Place flatnose pliers on top of the mark and bend both sides of the wire up at right angles. Trim the wire if necessary to make both sides the same length.

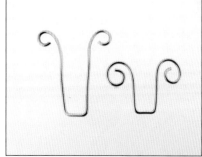

2. With roundnose and flatnose pliers, make open spirals on both ends. Work both ends alternately to keep them even.

TIP It's normal to use a lot of force to get a spiral started. To avoid marking the spiral, try using nylon-jaw or parallel-jaw pliers.

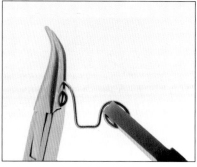

3. Hold one spiral with bentnose pliers while using the tip of the flatnose pliers to make a final turn in the opposite spiral.

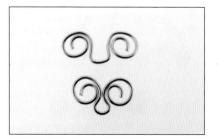

4. Repeat step 3 to finish the other spiral as shown. Note the point where the wire touches itself. Grasp both spirals between your thumb and index fingers and push them together to close the center gap.

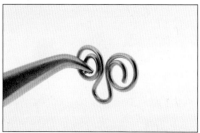

5. With the tip of the bentnose pliers, grasp the end of the wire and curve it in a slightly tighter spiral to tighten and secure the link. Repeat with the opposite spiral. Hammer flat. Make a total of five spiral links.

6. Cut 6" (15cm) of wire and make a double-ended spiral as you did for the choker project on p. 36. Grasp the spirals with your fingers and push them together so they touch in the center.

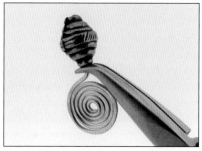

7. Cut 6" (15cm) of wire. Make a closed round spiral with five coils. String the GB. Place the tip of the bentnose pliers under the GB; this will leave a small gap between the loop and the spiral to allow for movement. Cut the wire. Hammer the spiral flat and make a loop perpendicular to the spiral's plane. Make a second round spiral component. Make three oval spiral components in a similar way.

8. Working from the spool, string a GB, a rondelle, an oval spiral, a rondelle, and a GB on the wire. Make a loop at each end. Hammer the loops flat. Make a total of two bead links using the round spiral components and two using the oval spiral components.

9. To make a spiral headpin, cut 4" (10cm) of wire. Make a three-coil closed spiral. Break the neck and hammer the spiral flat. String a 12mm coin bead and a GB. Trim the wire, make a loop, and hammer the loop flat. Make a total of four beaded spiral headpin components—two with 12mm coin beads and two with 15mm beads.

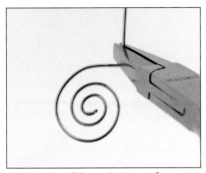

10. Cut two 5" (13cm) pieces of wire. Make a three-coil open spiral. With flatnose pliers, make a right-angle bend upward. Hammer the spiral flat. Make a second open-spiral component.

11. String a GB, trim the wire, and make a loop. Hammer the loop flat. Attach a beaded spiral headpin component to the open spiral. Attach the open spiral to the bottom of a spiral link.

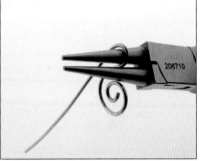

12. To make a squiggle unit, cut 4" (10cm) of wire. Grasp the end of the wire with roundnose pliers and make a two-coil open spiral. With roundnose pliers, grasp the wire where the spiral ends and bend the wire around and over the top jaw as shown.

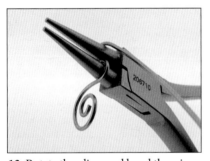

13. Rotate the pliers and bend the wire to curve in the opposite direction over the jaw. Repeat this action to make a third bend. Hammer the spiral flat. Make a loop and hammer the loop flat. Make a second squiggle unit.

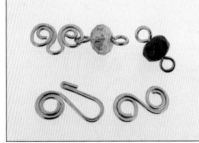

14. Prepare 14 bead links using rondelles, making sure the loops are on the same plane. Hammer the loops flat. Make a connector, a hook clasp, and three oval spirals as for the bracelet on p. 39. Hammer the spirals and curves on the components flat.

15. Work from the center to assemble the necklace. Make a bead link with the 18mm coin bead. Attach one loop to the bottom of a spiral link and the other to the double spiral. Attach an oval spiral to the bottom of the double spiral to finish the centerpiece.

16. On one side of the centerpiece, attach a round spiral bead link, an open-spiral component, a squiggle unit, a 15mm beaded spiral headpin component, an oval spiral bead link, and a chain made of seven bead links. Repeat this step on the other side of the centerpiece and attach the hook clasp to one end.

ANOTHER IDEA

Many of the
necklace components would make great earrings.

TIP

Close the inside loop of the open spirals so the beads can't wriggle out, especially if they are light.

PROJECT10
Jump ring bracelet

With this project, I want to dispel the idea that making jump rings is the equivalent of playing scales when learning the piano; in other words, tedious but necessary. Well-made, perfectly fitting jump rings perform a vital supporting role but can also be used to make a beautiful piece of jewelry in their own right. I used copper and silver rings, but you can explore many variations: thicker gauges, colored wires, and different size ratios. You'll love the silky smoothness of the rings on your skin.

Length: 7" (18cm)

WHAT YOU'LL NEED

- 30" (76cm) 18-gauge (1mm) silver wire
- 18" (46cm) 18-gauge (1mm) soft copper wire
- Wire cutters
- Bentnose pliers
- Flatnose pliers
- Roundnose pliers
- 10mm mandrel
- Bench block
- Chasing hammer
- Nylon-head mallet
- File
- Kitchen knife (optional)

Forming and using jump rings

Links are an important building block in wirework. For top-notch jewelry, links need to be well-formed and absolutely secure. They also create movement and articulation in your jewelry, making it fit and drape comfortably. Consider the purpose as you choose a shape and style for the links you use.

The simplest form of connection is the jump ring. Although commercially produced rings are commonly available in many gauges, metals, tempers, and diameters, it's very useful to know how to make your own. Consider the following points as you begin to make your own jump rings.

Gauge: A jump ring must be strong enough to remain firmly closed under pressure yet flexible enough so you can open it to connect it to other parts. Ideally, you should use 20-gauge (0.8mm) and thicker.

Temper: Half-hard is best, although you can begin with soft wire and work-harden it thoroughly by shaping, manipulating, and hammering it on the bench block. Soft wire is easier to coil but requires effort to harden.

Diameter: Remember that because the jump rings will link pieces, they need to have a diameter that's wide enough to accommodate the two parts with some room for movement. The size of the mandrel you use to form the jump rings determines their diameter.

Making jump rings is a two-part process: coiling and cutting. The coils must be uniform. You can coil around some type of mandrel or work directly on one jaw of the roundnose pliers (best when you need only a few rings). To trim the jump rings, be sure you have fine-tipped, sharp flush cutters because you'll use only the very tip of the cutters.

Poorly made jump rings can be the weakest link in any jewelry piece, so it's worth the effort to take your time and practice this skill. Your jewelry will stand the test of time with well-crafted links.

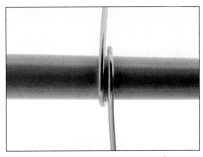

1. Measure and cut 18" (46cm) of copper wire or work off the spool. Run the wire through the polishing cloth several times until clean. Place the centerpoint of the wire on the center of the mandrel. Wrap the wire once tightly around the mandrel, making sure the coils are touching and perpendicular to the mandrel. Wrap until you reach the end of the wire. Because you work-hardened the wire as you wrapped, the end will be difficult to wrap; you can leave it straight.

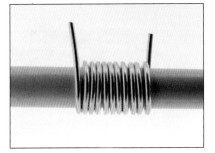

2. Turn the work over and wrap the other wire end around the mandrel. Slide the coiled wire to one end of the mandrel to remove it. If the coil is stuck, twist both ends in opposite directions to loosen it.

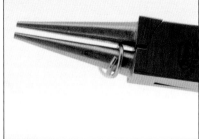

3. Use the same method to make the silver rings on a smaller mandrel or give the pliers method a try (you may want to do a trial run using copper, as I show in the photos). Place the tip of the wire just above the base of the jaw of the roundnose pliers and make a complete turn. (The first coil will not be used; be sure the second coil is formed at a perfect right angle to the jaw.) Check that the wire end is on the outside.

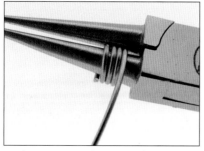

4. Place your nondominant thumb on the wire as you squeeze and rotate the pliers a quarter turn with your dominant hand. Repeat the movement to coil the wire. It's a quick, small motion, similar to ratcheting a screwdriver, while your nondominant thumb remains steady to shape the wire around the pliers.

It is sometimes difficult to cut just one ring without damaging the next. Slip a thin-bladed knife between each ring as you work and the problem is solved!

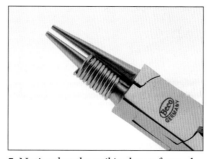

5. Notice that the coil is always formed at the widest part of the jaw, near the base. Make about 10 coils. (More than that and you risk misshapen rings.) Slip the coil off the pliers. Make four or five coils; you need 39 silver rings for the bracelet.

7. Flip the cutters so the cut end of the ring sits just inside the V of the beveled side. With the flat side toward you, cut the first ring. Both ends should now be flush-cut.

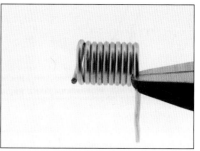

6. The cutters have one flush (flat) side and one beveled side. With the flat side of the cutters toward the coil, use the very tip of the cutters to cut only one ring at the point where the wire starts to coil.

8. As one end of the wire is flush-cut, the end left on the coil is beveled. The tiny peak needs to be trimmed with the flush side of the cutters. Continue in this way until all the rings are cut. Make 39 small silver rings and 13 large copper rings.

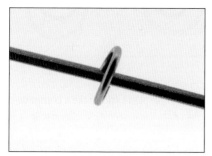

9. If the ring ends feel rough after cutting, run them along a file to smooth both sides at the same time.

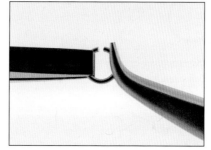

10. To work-harden the jump rings, open and close them sideways a few times using two pairs of pliers, and bringing the ends closer together with each move. End with open rings for this project.

11. Align the ends and close the rings. You now need to harden the jump rings a little more without distorting them. Strike them several times using a nylon-head mallet on a bench block.

   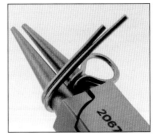

12. To make the hook clasp, cut 3" (7.5cm) of copper wire and mark the centerpoint. Make a U shape at that point, working at the base of the roundnose pliers.

13. With the flatnose pliers positioned slightly above the round jaw, squeeze the wire ends together. Hammer the loop flat.

14. Place the loop in the flatnose pliers and make a right-angle bend in both wires as shown.

15. Place the bend in the jaws of the roundnose pliers and use your fingers to bend both wires around one jaw toward the loop. Trim the ends to make them even.

16. Grasp both ends of the wire in the tips of the roundnose pliers and make a small loop.

17. Press the looped end down so only a small gap remains. There should be a slight resistance when the loop goes through the clasp so the bracelet is secure.

Using colored wire

with other metals creates a striking combination.

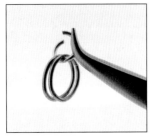 

18. Pick up two large copper rings with an open silver ring. Close the silver ring.

19. Attach two more silver rings. Continue linking a total of 12 copper rings with sets of silver rings. At one end, attach the clasp using three silver rings.

PROJECT 11

Figure-8 link necklace

Figure-8 links are much stronger than jump rings and are often used as the eye part of hook-and-eye clasps. In this project, you'll learn a simple way to shape the link that produces consistently good results. This design uses a twisted version of the link to show you how versatile it can be when you want to change the direction to attach a clasp, for instance. You can also make this design without the twist.

Length: 17½" (45cm)

WHAT YOU'LL NEED

- 55" (140cm) 18-gauge (1mm) wire
- 70" (180cm) 22-gauge (0.6mm) wire
- **3** 8mm focal beads
- **12** 6mm rondelle beads, color A
- **7** 6mm rondelle beads, color B
- **32** 2–3mm daisy spacers
- Wire cutters
- Bentnose pliers
- Chainnose pliers
- Flatnose pliers
- Roundnose pliers
- Bench block or anvil
- Chasing hammer

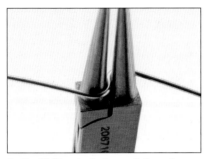

1. Cut 2" (5cm) of wire and place the centerpoint between the jaws of the roundnose pliers about a wire width from the base.

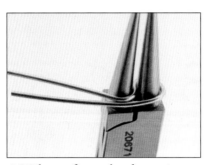

2. With your fingers, bend one wire around one jaw so it rests immediately below the wire in the other jaw.

3. Flip the pliers 180 degrees and bend the opposite wire end so it rests immediately on top of the wire in the other jaw.

4. Remove the link from the pliers. Slip one loop over one jaw as shown and bend the wire around to complete the loop.

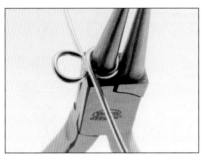

5. Remove the loop from the jaw. Place the other loop over the jaw and repeat step 4.

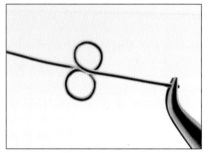

6. Remove the link from the pliers. It should look like a fat figure 8 with two tails.

7. It's not often that you'll cut the wire with the bevel side of the cutters, but here you need to get as close as possible to the top wire. Place the flat side of the cutters against the middle of the 8 and cut the wire.

8. Flip the cutters and trim the tip of the wire in a slight wedge so it fits neatly against the middle wire. Repeat steps 7 and 8 on the other wire end.

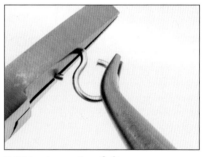

9. Using two pairs of pliers, open one loop of the S and file the end of the wire. Close the loop and repeat on the other side. Hammer the curves to flatten and strengthen them. Close the loops again if necessary.

 TIP To make smaller figure-8 links, mark the pliers higher up the jaw and make your loops at that point.

10. To twist a link, grasp the entire top loop with flatnose pliers and the bottom loop with chainnose pliers.

11. Twist both pliers to form a right angle. Close the loops. Make a total of 22 twisted links.

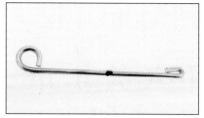

12. To make a simple, useful variation on the hook closure, cut a 1¾" (4.5cm) piece of 18-gauge (1mm) wire. Make a loop at one end and a tight U at the other end, both facing the same way. Measure and mark the centerpoint.

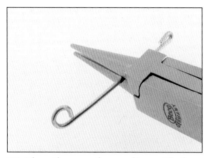

13. Place the roundnose pliers with the mark just showing on the loop side. With your thumb on the loop end and your index finger on the U end, push the ends down around the jaw and toward each other.

14. Hammer the curve and the outside of the loop flat. Cut a 4" (10cm) piece of 20-gauge (0.8mm) wire. Make three oval spiral headpins. Hammer the spirals flat. String a daisy spacer, a color-A rondelle, and a daisy spacer. Make a wrapped loop. Make a total of two spiral dangles in color A and one in color B.

15. On 5" (13cm) of 22-gauge (0.6mm) wire, string a color-A rondelle, a daisy spacer, a focal bead, a spacer, and an A. Make a wrapped loop at each end. Make a total of three.

16. On 4" (10cm) of 22-gauge (0.6mm) wire, string a spacer, a rondelle, and a spacer. Make a wrapped loop at each end. Make four in color A and six in color B.

17. Attach a link at each end of a focal bead set, and then to the bottom ring of the figure-8 link, attach a link, a spiral bead dangle, two links, a spiral bead dangle, three links, and a spiral bead dangle. From the pendant, attach a link, a color-B bead link, a link, a focal-bead set, a link, a B bead link, a link, an A bead link, and a link. Repeat the pattern until you reach the desired length. Repeat the sequence to create the other end of the necklace and attach the hook closure.

ANOTHER IDEA

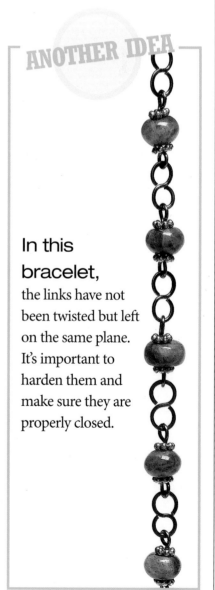

In this bracelet,

the links have not been twisted but left on the same plane. It's important to harden them and make sure they are properly closed.

PROJECT 12
Double spiral-link bracelet

Very strong and elegant, double-spiral links form an integral part of this design. To lengthen or shorten the bracelet, vary the size of the spirals. This project also shows how to make a spiral bead cap from wire—an elegant solution to cover large holes or finish irregularly shaped beads.

Length: 8½" (22cm)
WHAT YOU'LL NEED

- 30" (80cm) 22-gauge (0.6mm) soft wire
- 30" (80cm) 18-gauge (1mm) soft wire
- **3** 30 x 24mm flat oval beads
- Wire cutters
- Bentnose pliers
- Flatnose pliers
- Roundnose pliers
- Bench block and guard
- Chasing hammer
- 10mm and 14mm GBs

1. Clean and cut 7" (18cm) of 18-gauge (1mm) wire. Mark the centerpoint and place the wire between the jaws of the roundnose pliers, as close to the top as is comfortable. Use your fingers to bend each wire end around the jaw in opposite directions.

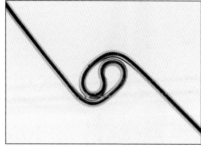

2. Remove the wire from the pliers and place it flat on your work surface. Check if all of the shaped wire is on the same plane; gently nudge the wire in place with your fingers if necessary.

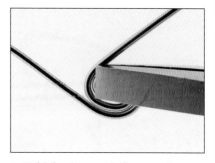

3. Hold the shape with flatnose pliers adjacent to, but not touching, the wire end. Slowly begin to spiral the wire end against the center shape, keeping the spiral flat with no gaps. Reposition the pliers frequently as you work your way around. Move to the other wire end and begin to spiral it in the same way.

4. As you move from working with one end to the other, reposition the pliers so you have a firm grip on the spiral.

5. Spiral around the center shape four times with each end. Finish with both ends pointing in opposite directions as shown. Trim both ends using a 10mm guide bead.

6. Using roundnose pliers, form a loop on each side of the spiral. Do not break the necks on these loops. Hammer the whole link carefully. Make another spiral link.

7. Cut a 10" (26cm) piece of 18-gauge (1mm) wire. String an oval bead and make a wrapped loop on both sides, coiling three times around the neck. Do not trim the wire ends.

8. Hold the loop firmly in the bentnose pliers. Holding the wire about 2" (5cm) away from the bead, wrap the wire around the top of the bead with your fingers. Reposition the pliers every half-turn.

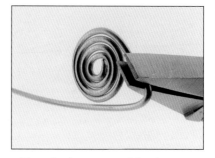

9. To make the swan-neck hook, cut 7" (18cm) of 18-gauge (1mm) wire. Make a four-rotation spiral. Place the tip of the flatnose pliers on the wire and bend it to make an acute angle as shown. Push the wire end against the spiral.

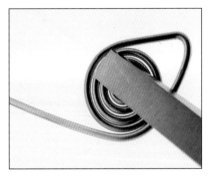

10. Grasp the whole spiral in the flatnose pliers and bend as shown to form the neck.

11. Place the wire about three-quarters of the way down in the jaws of the roundnose pliers jaws. Wrap the wire end around the jaw toward the spiral.

12. Flush-cut the wire, aligning the cut with the outside of the spiral as shown. Make a small outward loop. Hammer the hook loop and the spiral.

13. To make the eye part of the clasp, repeat steps 9 and 10. String a 14mm GB, trim the wire, and make a large loop. Hammer the work. Grasp the large loop with flatnose pliers and bend it at a right angle to the spiral. Close tightly.

14. Make two twisted figure-8 links. To assemble the bracelet, connect components in this order: swan-neck hook, figure-8 link, bead, double spiral, bead, double spiral, bead, figure-8 link, eye part of the clasp.

ANOTHER IDEA

Use the double-spiral link to add design interest to a simple pair of long, dangly earrings.

PROJECT13
Clover leaf earrings

This is an elegant version of chandelier earrings. All of the main components are made with simple loops that create clover leaf headpins. You could use crystals and connect even more dangles to the smaller headpins. The earring wires are so easy to make, you'll never want to buy commercial earring wires again!

Length: 2½" (6cm)

WHAT YOU'LL NEED

- 35" (90cm) 20-gauge (0.8mm) wire
- 4" (10cm) 21-gauge (0.75mm) or 20-gauge (0.8mm) wire
- **8** 10mm focal beads
- **16** 4mm metal spacers
- Wire cutters
- Chainnose pliers
- Flatnose pliers
- Roundnose pliers
- ⁵⁄₁₆" (8mm) mandrel
- Bench block and guard
- Chasing hammer
- File or wire rounder
- **2** 10mm GBs

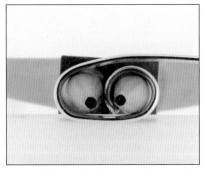

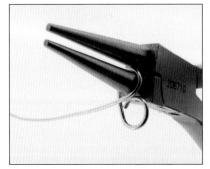

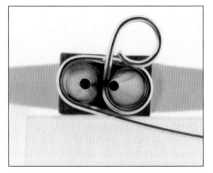

1. Cut 5" (13cm) of 20-gauge (0.8mm) wire. Mark the pliers one wire width from the bottom of the jaw, place the wire in the jaws at that point, and make a closed loop. Bring the wire around the opposite jaw as shown.

2. Remove the work from the pliers. Working at the same point as in step 1, place the unfinished loop over one jaw and complete the loop.

3. Remove the work from the pliers, flip it over, and place the same loop on the jaw, this time with the wire tail going under the loop. Make a loop around the other jaw as shown. Remove the work from the pliers.

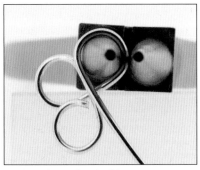

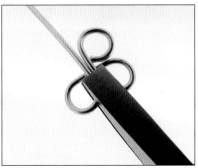

4. Place the unfinished loop over one jaw and complete the loop.

5. The wires may be slightly on top of each other; use the tip of the flatnose pliers to flatten them so they are on the same plane.

6. Bend the wire at the base of the clover shape with the tip of the flatnose pliers so it looks like a stem. Hammer only the tips of the loops. Make a second identical clover shape. Follow steps 1–6 to make six small clover leaves using 4" (10cm) of wire and working closer to the tip of the roundnose pliers jaws to shape smaller loops.

TIP Turn this design into a link by trimming the wire at the end of step 5. The link is particularly useful for attaching a clasp to a two-strand bracelet or necklace.

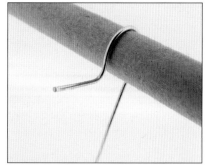

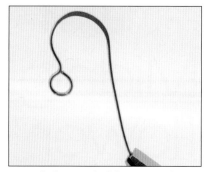

7. To make the earring wires: Cut 2" (5cm) of wire. File the ends until they are smooth. Place the GB on the end and bend the wire at a right angle below the bead. Remove the GB.

8. Hold the wire on the mandrel with your thumb at the bend. Curve the other end three-quarters of the way around the mandrel.

9. On the bent end of the wire, make an inward loop. Hammer the top of the curve flat. Grasp ⅛" (3mm) from the end of the wire with flatnose pliers and bend at a 45-degree angle. Make a second earring wire.

10. On the large clover leaf headpin, string a metal spacer, a focal bead, a spacer, and a GB. Trim the wire, remove the GB, and make a loop. Repeat this step for a second large headpin and four small ones.

String the two remaining clover headpins in the same way, and then, measure and mark ½" (13mm) above the metal spacer to make a long dangle. Place the flatnose pliers under the mark. String the GB, trim the wire above the bead, and remove the GB. Make a loop. Make a second long dangle. Assemble the earrings by opening and closing the loops (see photo on p. 55).

ANOTHER IDEA

Clover links (see tip) make an interesting bracelet or choker. The large loops are formed at the base of the roundnose pliers.

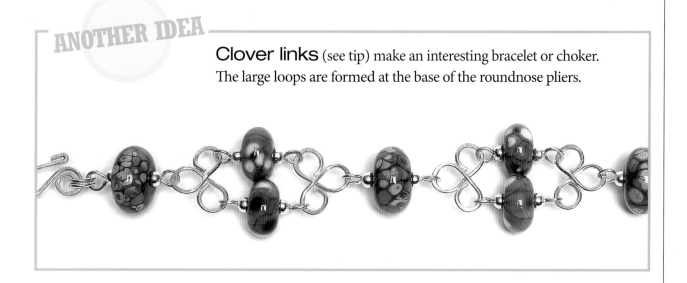

PROJECT 14
Midnight flower bracelet

Length: 6¾" (17cm)

WHAT YOU'LL NEED

- 45" (115cm) 20-gauge (0.8mm) wire
- **13** 6mm beads
- Wire cutters
- Flatnose pliers
- Roundnose pliers
- Bench block and guard
- Chasing hammer
- 10mm GB

These flower-shaped links are a strong and pretty way to connect two rows of bead links. They are a little bit tricky to make because you have to ensure that the wires lie flat against each other and the loops are the same size. Shaping the links will build on the clover design learned in the previous project; you'll add one more loop and remove the wire tail. I used black craft wire to highlight the light color of the pearls.

TIP If you are worried about marring the wire, use nylon-jaw pliers instead of flatnose pliers to flatten the work.

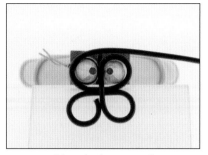

1. Cut 3½" (9cm) of wire. Mark one jaw in your favorite way to make a large loop. Follow steps 1–5 of the previous project, making a clover shape. Flip the work over, place the last loop made on the unmarked jaw, and bend the wire around the marked jaw.

2. Remove the work from the pliers, place the unfinished loop on the marked jaw, and finish the loop.

3. Use the tip of the flatnose pliers to gently flatten the wire so the lines and curves align neatly. Holding the tail in your fingers, hammer only the tips of the loops to flatten them slightly, being careful to avoid overlaps in the wire.

4. Trim the tail with the tip of the cutters in the center of the flower. You can lift the tail up a little to make a clean cut and then flatten it with pliers.

5. Prepare 13 bead links using pearls, two clover links (see previous project), five flower links, and a hook clasp (as in Project 10, p. 45)

6. To assemble, attach a double row of bead links to the flower connectors, ending with beads on both ends. Attach a clover link to the last two beads on each end. On one end, attach one bead link and the hook.

ANOTHER IDEA

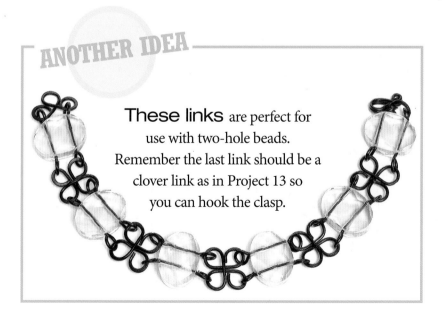

These links are perfect for use with two-hole beads. Remember the last link should be a clover link as in Project 13 so you can hook the clasp.

TIP

Clover and flower links are just a sampling of the various connectors you can make. Experiment with scraps of wire and create a few of your own!

PROJECT 15
Stylish brooch

This classic design, sometimes called a fibula, can be dressed in a variety of ways. I love crystal drop beads because they are just so sparkly. Unfortunately, they usually have a horizontal channel very close to their fragile tops and are all too easy to break (here I speak from painful experience!). You'll learn a safe way to wrap them with thin wire using your fingers rather than tools. This delicate-yet-strong bail will avoid stressing the edges of the hole while protecting the tip.

Width: 2⅜" (6cm)

WHAT YOU'LL NEED

- 16" (40cm) 18-gauge (1mm) half-hard wire
- 16" (40cm) 26-gauge (0.4mm) wire
- 8" (20cm) 20-gauge (0.8mm) wire
- 15 x 10mm drop bead
- **2** 12mm crystal drops
- **2** 6mm beads
- **2** 5mm metal beads
- **2** 4mm beads
- **2** 3mm metal beads
- **6** 2–3mm daisy spacers
- Wire cutters
- Bentnose pliers
- Flatnose pliers
- Roundnose pliers
- Nylon-jaw pliers
- Bench block
- Chasing hammer
- 8mm mandrel
- File
- 10mm GB

1. Cut 8" (20cm) of 26-gauge (0.4mm) wire. String the crystal drop to the center of the wire. Using your fingers, bend the wires toward and across each other, and pinch them together just above the bead. Using bentnose pliers, bend both wires forward in a right angle over the bead.

2. Place roundnose pliers at the bend and make a loop, shaping both wires at the same time. Keep the loop on the jaw and rotate the pliers so you can begin wrapping both wires around the neck. Make sure the wires remain parallel.

3. Still holding the wires firmly in the pliers, continue wrapping, moving down and over the bead. Trim both wires at the back of the work and gently flatten them against the bead using nylon-jaw pliers. Wrap a second crystal drop the same way.

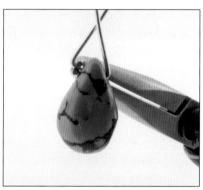

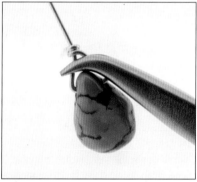

4. Cut 4" (10cm) of 20-gauge (0.8mm) wire and mark it at 2" (5cm). Bend the wire at a 45-degree angle with flatnose pliers. Slide the bead to the bend. Place the tip of the bentnose pliers against the bead on the other side. Bend the wire toward the bead, mirroring the first angle.

5. Bend one wire end up and the other across as shown.

6. Hold the triangle firmly with bentnose pliers while making three wraps with the horizontal wire. Trim. Use the GB to measure and cut the upright wire. Make a loop perpendicular to the triangle.

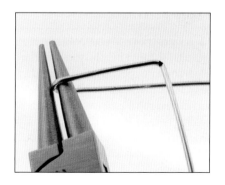

7. To straighten the 18-gauge (1mm) wire and make it springy, run it through the polishing cloth several times and then through nylon-jaw pliers. Cut 10" (25cm) of wire. Using flatnose pliers, make a right-angle bend 1¼" (3cm) from the end. Use roundnose pliers to make a hairpin curve as shown 1¼" (3cm) from the right-angle bend.

8. Hold the curved shape tightly in the flatnose pliers, make three wraps, and trim the wire end. This will be the catch for the pin. Hammer the catch, avoiding the wraps. Bend the end at a slight angle using flatnose pliers.

9. Using your fingers, bend the catch around the mandrel.

Choose a long

focal bead for a simple, quick-to-make brooch or make three or more loops and dangle some charms. Brooches can be whimsical, so don't be afraid to choose a theme as I did with my beachcomber finds.

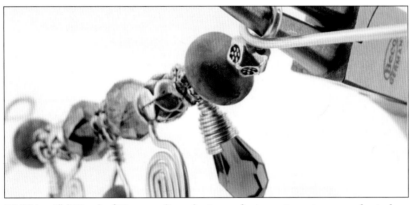

10. Using 3" (7.5cm) of 18-gauge (1mm) wire, make two mirror-image oval spirals with loops at the top. Hammer the ovals flat. On the pin base, string: 3mm metal bead, 4mm bead, daisy spacer, wrapped crystal drop, daisy spacer, 5mm metal bead, left spiral, 6mm bead, daisy spacer, crystal drop, daisy spacer, 6mm bead, right spiral, 5mm metal bead, daisy spacer, crystal drop, daisy spacer, 4mm bead, 3mm metal bead. Place the roundnose pliers tight against the beads and make a loop toward the beads. Make a second half-loop over the first.

11. With your fingers, gently curve the wire holding the beads. Bend the loose wire (the pin) up and down gently a few times to make it springy. Trim the pin so it has a comfortable clearance from the catch.

12. A wire's trimmed end looks like a cylinder. To finish the pin, you'll file the edges and turn the end into a pointed cone: Place the file flat on the work surface and rub the wire over the file, holding the end at a 30-degree angle and slowly rolling the wire to create a point. Repeat with a nail file to smooth any rough spots.

PROJECT 16
Picasso jasper necklace

Length: 20" (51cm)

WHAT YOU'LL NEED

- 11' (33m) 18-gauge (1mm) soft wire
- 16" (40cm) 22-gauge (0.6mm) soft wire
- Pendant bead
- 20mm focal bead
- **15** 8mm beads
- Wire cutters
- Bentnose pliers
- Flatnose pliers
- Roundnose pliers
- Bench block or anvil
- Chasing hammer
- Guard
- 10mm and 12mm GBs

I love the pattern and the colors of this beautiful fan-shaped jasper bead, but it has a large, unsightly hole. The fancy bail in this project suspends the pendant bead securely and lets it move freely while disguising its single fault. The oval caged bead adds interest and stability to the centerpiece.

1. To make the bail: Cut 8" (20cm) of 18-gauge (1mm) wire. Make a right-angle bend in the center with flatnose pliers. String the pendant bead next to the bend, place the tip of the bentnose pliers on the horizontal wire against the bead, and bend to form a U shape. Bend both wires over the bead to form an X.

2. Bend the longer end in a right angle and bend the short end straight up. Hold the triangle with the tip of bentnose pliers. Wrap the longer end once around the upright wire and down over the front of the bead.

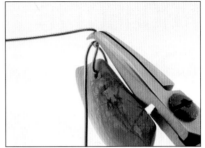

3. Place the tip of the bentnose pliers above the wrap. Bend the wire in a right angle to the front of the bead.

4. Using roundnose pliers, make a wrapped loop with the tail ending at the front of the bead.

5. Make a spiral with the tail of the top wire and center it below the loop. Using the tail of the lower wire, make a second spiral in the opposite direction until the spiral reaches the base of the first spiral. Manipulate both spirals with your fingers until you are satisfied with their placement. Pull the loop backwards while pushing the spirals against the bead to stabilize. Hammer the loop.

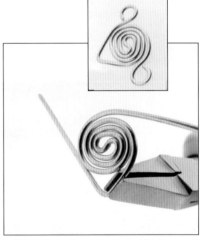

6. To make a three-way spiral link, cut 6" (15cm) of 18-gauge (1mm) wire. Make a double spiral. In the middle of the last turn as shown, make a notch with the flatnose pliers. (If you like, you can use roundnose pliers to make a rounded notch instead.) Continue forming the spiral and make a loop at each end (see photo with step 11). Hammer flat. Make a total of three three-way spiral links.

TIP Don't be afraid to use different gauges of wire in the same piece. Use the gauge that is appropriate for the beads as long as you don't compromise the strength of the whole piece.

7. To make a wire cage for the oval bead, cut 10" (25cm) of 22-gauge (0.6mm) wire. Mark the center. Spiral both ends in opposite directions until they almost meet. Make the center holes of the spirals large enough to accommodate 18-gauge (1mm) wire. Transform the spirals into cones by placing the tip of the roundnose pliers in each center hole and pushing down with your fingers evenly.

8. Manipulate the cones so the large openings face each other as shown.

9. Slip the 20mm bead inside the cage. Make a bead link working off the spool of 18-gauge (1mm) wire. Hammer the loops.

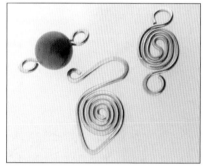

10. For one 8mm bead, repeat steps 7–9 using 6" (15cm) of 22-gauge (0.6mm) wire. If the wire between the cones is loose, make a tiny Z-shape bend using the tips of the roundnose pliers.

11. Also prepare a swan neck clasp (see Project 12, p. 52), 14 bead links, and 10 three-row double spirals each using 5" (12.5cm) of 18-gauge (1mm) wire. Hammer all loops and spirals.

12. Follow the photo on p. 63 for the placement of the components. Connect them by opening and closing loops, beginning with the clasp.

ANOTHER IDEA

To make a big, bold statement, you could use very large beads such as these 18mm gemstone beauties. The wire bead caps really liven them up. These Z-bends were made with the tip of flatnose pliers. They add a decorative touch and tighten the wire neatly around the bead.

PROJECT17
Pearl cluster earrings

This project shows you how to make three different types of simple headpins: folded, paddle, and squiggle. Making your own headpins allows you to choose the metal, the gauge, the temper, and the length you like. If, like me, you love freshwater pearls, you will find that making your own headpins is a valuable skill, because pearls tend to have very small holes that seldom fit commercial headpins.

Length: 2⅜" (6cm)

WHAT YOU'LL NEED

- 35" (90cm) 20-gauge (0.8mm) wire
- 30" (75cm) 26-gauge (0.4mm) soft craft wire
- **8** 6mm crystals
- **6** 5–6mm chocolate pearls
- **6** 5–6mm white pearls
- **8** bead caps
- Wire cutters
- Bentnose pliers
- Flatnose pliers
- Roundnose pliers
- ⅜" (9mm) mandrel
- Bench block or anvil
- Chasing hammer
- 10mm GB

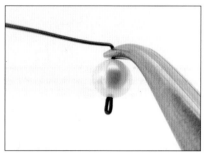

1. To make a folded headpin, cut 5" (12cm) of 26-gauge (0.4mm) craft wire. Fold and flatten the tip with flatnose pliers. Cut the tip of the folded wire in a wedge shape so the pearl will fit neatly over it.

2. String a white pearl on the headpin until it is firmly seated. Grasp the wire above the bead with the tip of the bentnose pliers and use your fingers to bend the wire at a right angle. Make a loop with roundnose pliers and do not trim the wire tail.

3. Hold the loop with the bentnose pliers and wrap the wire down the neck. When you reach the pearl, gently wrap the wire against the top of the pearl as shown. Hold the wire at some distance to the pearl and wrap very slowly. Cut the wire in a wedge shape against the pearl. Make a total of six white pearl dangles on folded headpins.

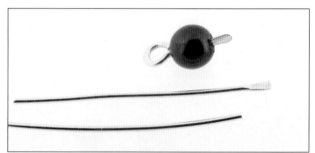

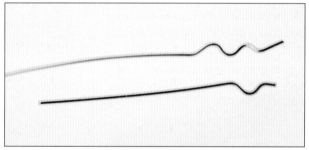

4. To make a paddle headpin, cut 2" (5cm) of 20-gauge (0.8mm) wire. Place one end on the bench block and hammer about ⅛" (3mm) of the end flat. The wire end will be wider than the bead hole and will keep the pearl in place. File the paddle end until smooth. String a chocolate pearl and make a loop. Make a total of six dangles on paddle headpins.

5. To make squiggle headpins, cut two lengths of 20-gauge (0.8mm) wire: 2½" (6cm) for a long squiggle and 2" (5cm) for the short version. Use roundnose and/or flatnose pliers to make a few bends on one end.

6. Hammer the bends flat and file the ends. String a crystal, a bead cap, and a GB. Trim the wire, remove the GB, and make a loop. Make a total of two long and four short dangles on squiggle headpins.

TIP

Choose your headpin length based on how many beads you want to string, and determine what gauge to use by the size of the bead holes. If the bead hole is really large, string a small seed or metal bead first.

7. Make twelve ³⁄₁₆" (5mm) jump rings from the 20-gauge (0.8mm) wire. Attach a jump ring to a long squiggle dangle. *Pick up a new jump ring and string a white pearl dangle, the previous jump ring, and a chocolate pearl dangle, and close the jump ring. Pick up a new jump ring and string a squiggle dangle and the previous jump ring. Close the jump ring.* Repeat the sequence between the asterisks, ending with a chocolate and a white pearl dangle.

8. For each beaded earring wire, cut 2" (5cm) of 20-gauge (0.8mm) wire. Use the GB to bend the wire at a right angle and make a loop at one end. String a crystal and a bead cap. Place the wire on the mandrel and bend it around firmly with your fingers. Grasp the end with flatnose pliers and bend it at a 45-degree angle. Hammer the bend. Attach the beaded dangles to the earring wire loop.

9. Assemble a second earring.

ANOTHER IDEA

Make a dainty

matching pendant by adding as many dangles as you want and hanging it on a chain or pretty ribbon. To make a cone, follow the instructions for making jump rings on roundnose pliers, but place the end of the wire on the inside. Your cone will have the size and shape of the pliers' jaw.

PROJECT 18

All my heart necklace

The heart motif is always a very popular design in jewelry. It appeals to all romantics and never seems to go out of fashion. In this project, one technique is adapted to perform many different functions. By simply altering the size of the heart, you can make a headpin, a central connector, a link, or a clasp.

Length: 21" (53cm)

WHAT YOU'LL NEED

- 25" (65cm) 18-gauge (1mm) wire
- 70" (175cm) 20-gauge (0.8mm) wire
- **15** 4mm metal spacers
- **9** 12mm turquoise focal beads
- **17** 5 x 8mm turquoise rondelle beads
- 25mm drop bead
- **5** 14mm metal hearts
- **19** bead caps
- Wire cutters
- Bentnose pliers
- Flatnose pliers
- Roundnose pliers
- Bench block and guard
- Chasing hammer
- ³⁄₁₆" (4.5mm) mandrel or size 7 knitting needle (US/UK)
- 12mm GB

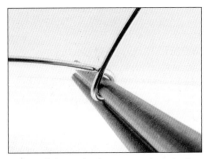

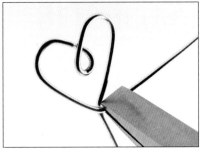

1. Cut 6" (15cm) of 20-gauge (0.8mm) wire. Measure and mark 2" (5cm) from an end. Place the mark about a quarter of the way down the jaws and bend the ends toward each other to make a loop as shown.

2. Mark the pliers about three-quarters of the way down the jaws so your hearts will be consistent. Place the loop at that point between the jaws without squeezing. Holding the shape down with a thumb, bend each wire end around the jaw and toward the other. Take care not to squash the center loop.

3. Place flatnose pliers on the long end at the base of the heart. Straighten it slightly so it aligns with the loop. Bend the short end up at a right angle to the first.

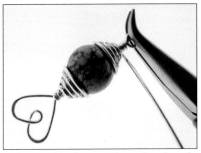

4. Hold the base of the heart in the bentnose pliers and wrap the short end around the stem three times and trim. Hammer the heart's curves (but not the center loop).

5. String a bead cap, a 12mm bead, and a bead cap. Make a wrapped loop. Make a total of eight bead-and-heart links. Make a clasp in a similar way, using a small rondelle instead of a large bead.

TIP

Using wire thicker than 20-gauge (0.8mm), bead hole permitting, would allow you to use a simple loop rather than a wrapped loop for the links.

ANOTHER IDEA

Make a pendant

with a heart connector and hang three drop beads for a pretty look. Use lighter beads and a smaller heart for a lovely pair of earrings.

6. Make the focal heart link in the same way, but form larger curves on the base of the roundnose pliers. For the tiny heart headpin, use 4" (10cm) of wire and form the curve using the tip of the jaws. Using 18-gauge (1mm) wire, prepare 10 sets of bead links made with a rondelle, a metal spacer, and a rondelle, and five metal heart links that include a metal spacer.

7. To make the hook clasp, cut 4" (10cm) of 18-gauge (1mm) wire. Make a one-and-a-half loop in the center as you did in Project 15, p. 60.

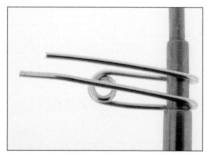

8. Measure ⅝" (1.5cm) from the end of the loop and bend both ends over the mandrel at that point. Trim the ends just above the loop.

9. Form a small loop at each wire end. As you form the loop, push down to curve the hook end slightly. Assemble the necklace starting with the pendant set of drop, metal heart, and heart centerpiece. Follow the photo on p. 69 for the remaining assembly.

TIP Push the clasp hooks together so they fit neatly on either side of the heart's central loop with a small amount of resistance. This secure style of clasp will work for many other projects as well.

PROJECT19
Secure earring wires

Do you have a collection of orphan earrings? You will appreciate this project, which shows how to make earring wires with a safety catch. You'll get the best results using sterling silver half-hard wire, but you can also use soft sterling silver wire if you condition and harden it to hold its shape. The measurements given are for the length of the earring wire only. Feel free to alter the size and add any type of dangle or embellishment you'd like!

Length: ⅞" (2cm), 1⅛" (3cm)

WHAT YOU'LL NEED

For the simple earrings:
- 5" (13cm) 20- or 21-gauge (0.75 or 0.8mm) sterling silver wire
- Assortment of beads and charms, 3–7mm

For the decorated earrings:
- 7" (18cm) 20- or 21-gauge (0.75 or 0.8mm) sterling silver wire
- Assortment of beads and charms, 3–10mm

For both styles:
- Wire cutters
- Bentnose pliers
- Flatnose pliers
- Roundnose pliers
- Nylon-jaw pliers
- Bench block or anvil
- Chasing hammer
- ⁵⁄₁₆" (8mm) mandrel
- File
- Wire rounder (optional)

simple

decorated

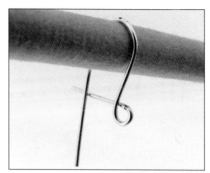

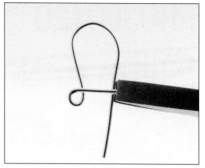

1. For each simple earring wire, cut 2½" (5cm) of 20-gauge (0.8mm) wire. Clean and straighten. Mark the wire at ½" (13mm). Grasp the wire at the mark about a third of the way down the jaws of the roundnose pliers and make a complete loop.

2. Mark the long end of the wire ½" (13mm) from the loop. Center the mark over the mandrel and use your fingers to bend the wire around the mandrel as shown.

3. Grasp the last ⅛" (4mm) of the short end of the wire in the flatnose pliers. Bend wire in a tiny hook, just long enough to hold the vertical wire in place. Trim if necessary.

ANOTHER IDEA

4. Trim the vertical wire ⅜" (10mm) down from the hook. Bend the wire end at a 45-degree angle.

5. Hammer the top curve to harden and flatten slightly. Use a file (or a wire rounder) to smooth the wire ends. Open and close the earring wire gently a few times until the wire feels springy. Attach your choice of bead dangles.

TIP

6. For each decorated earring wire, cut a 3½" (9cm) piece of wire. Make a loop as in step 1. String beads for about ¾" (2cm). Bend the wire around the mandrel just above the beads and complete the earring as in steps 3–5.

Smoothing the tip of the earring wire is very important for the wearer. If you make a lot of earrings, invest in a wire rounder (also called a cup bur). After you round the wire end by rotating it in the cup of this little tool, spend some time smoothing the metal with a fine file or sandpaper using gentle, feathery motions until you can feel no burs with your fingertip.

Experiment with various shapes of beads or a cluster of small looped beads that ends with a single bead so the clusters can't escape!

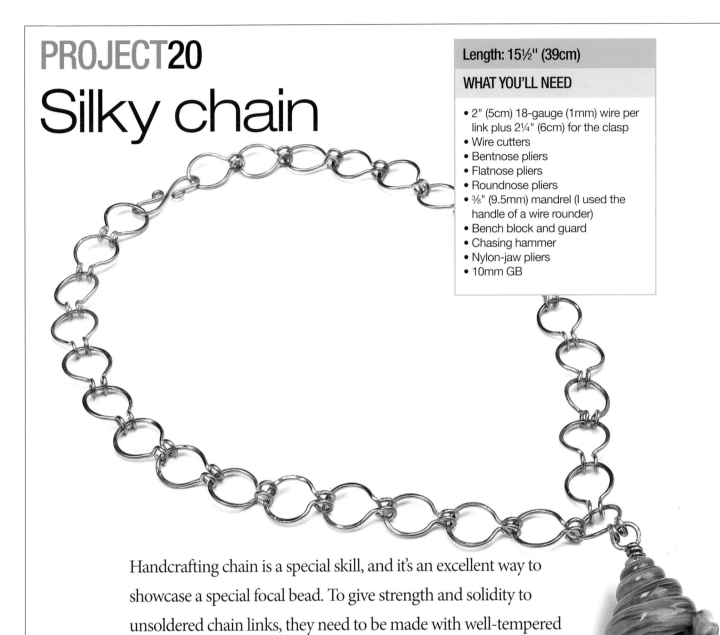

PROJECT20
Silky chain

Length: 15½" (39cm)

WHAT YOU'LL NEED

- 2" (5cm) 18-gauge (1mm) wire per link plus 2¼" (6cm) for the clasp
- Wire cutters
- Bentnose pliers
- Flatnose pliers
- Roundnose pliers
- ⅜" (9.5mm) mandrel (I used the handle of a wire rounder)
- Bench block and guard
- Chasing hammer
- Nylon-jaw pliers
- 10mm GB

Handcrafting chain is a special skill, and it's an excellent way to showcase a special focal bead. To give strength and solidity to unsoldered chain links, they need to be made with well-tempered and thick-gauge wire. This project uses bronze wire, a copper alloy that contains a small percentage of phosphorus and tin. The bronze wire has a lovely, mellow color and is also very strong. This project includes a versatile S-clasp that can be fastened at either end.

TIP Other metals will work just as well for this chain because the linking loops are formed in opposite directions and hammered to give them extra strength. The mandrel size indicated will make a ⁷⁄₁₆" (11mm) diameter link, but feel free to experiment with other sizes and also change the length of the necklace.

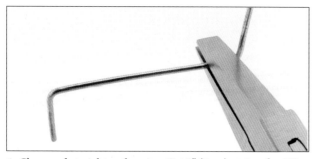

1. Clean and straighten the wire. Cut 2" (5cm), string the GB, place flatnose pliers under the bead, remove the bead, and bend the wire in a right angle against the pliers. Do the same at the other end, but make the bend in the opposite direction.

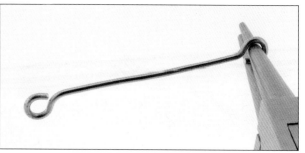

2. Make a loop at each end with openings on opposite sides of the wire. This will greatly strengthen the chain and help keep the links closed. Hammer both loops flat.

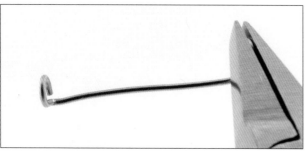

3. With flatnose pliers, bend each loop at a right angle so the loops face each other.

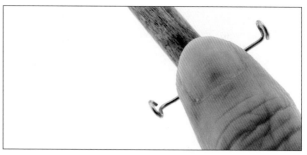

4. Use your thumb to hold the wire shape on the mandrel with the loops pointed up.

5. With your other thumb and forefinger, push the two loops down and around the mandrel. Try to do this in one fluid motion without twisting the ring. Don't worry about the direction of loops at this stage.

6. Hold the link with the straight edge of the guard to protect the loops. Hammer the ring using the ball of the hammer to add texture. If you prefer a smooth look, use the flat face of the hammer.

7. Use flatnose pliers to straighten the loops as shown. Make a total of 29 links (more if you want a longer chain and fewer for a bracelet). Make the loops of each link the same distance apart.

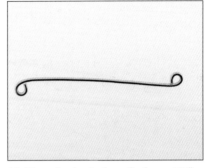

8. To connect the links, open each of the loops sideways. Slip a new ring under the open right loop and then bring it down between the loops and up through the left open loop (as if it were on a hinge). Close and straighten the loops. Make two chains of 14 links each.

9. Connect the two chains with the final link as shown. This center link is now a bail that can suspend a bead or pendant. Thoroughly inspect the chain to make sure all the loops are straight and closed.

10. To make the S-clasp, flush-cut 2¼" (5.7cm) of wire. With the tip of the pliers, make a small P-shaped loop at each end. Orient the loops in opposite directions.

TIP

These instructions are designed to give the pendant its own link. If you prefer to have the chain links going in one direction only, simply omit step 9.

11. Grasp the loop at the base of the roundnose pliers and bend the wire all the way around the jaw in the opposite direction of the curve of the loop.

12. Repeat step 11 with the other end to form an S shape. Carefully hammer the curves flat and adjust the ends if necessary to tighten. Attach the clasp to the necklace.

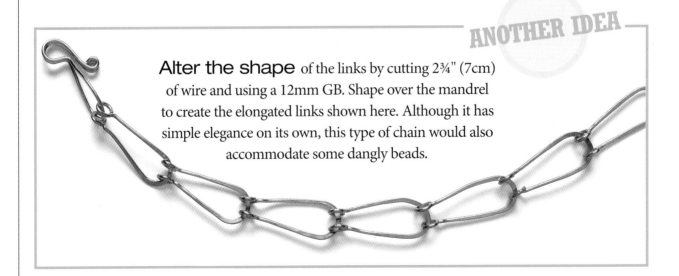

ANOTHER IDEA

Alter the shape of the links by cutting 2¾" (7cm) of wire and using a 12mm GB. Shape over the mandrel to create the elongated links shown here. Although it has simple elegance on its own, this type of chain would also accommodate some dangly beads.

PROJECT21
Hey presto! ring

This ring is very quick and easy to make, hence its name. A ring is one of the few pieces of jewelry that requires precise measuring, but because this design is open, you'll enjoy some flexibility in adjusting its size. It's important that a ring retains its shape, so hardening the wire thoroughly is crucial. With such a heavy gauge of wire as this, getting a grip to start the spirals is much more challenging. If you find it too difficult, try making this style in 18-gauge (1mm) wire first.

WHAT YOU'LL NEED

- Finger circumference plus 2½" (6cm) 16-gauge (1.25mm) wire
- 39" (1m) 26-gauge (0.4mm) wire
- Wire cutters
- Flatnose pliers
- Roundnose pliers
- Nylon-jaw pliers
- Ring mandrel
- Bench block or anvil
- Chasing hammer
- Nylon-head mallet
- Fine-point scissors

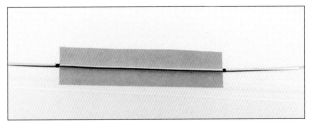

1. Cut a ½ x 3" (1.3 x 8cm) strip of paper. Wrap it around your finger knuckle so it fits snugly. Holding the strip in place with your thumb, use fine-point scissors to cut through both thicknesses in a straight line where the strip overlaps. The strip of paper represents your ring size. Working from the wire spool, measure and mark 1¼" (3.2cm) from the end of the wire. Place the strip of paper on the mark and make another mark where the strip ends. Measure 1¼" (3.2cm) from that mark and cut the wire at this point.

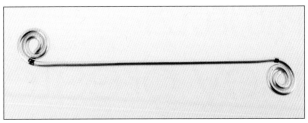

2. Clean and straighten the wire using nylon-jaw pliers. File the ends smooth. On each end, make a tight spiral that finishes at the mark. Face the spirals in opposite directions.

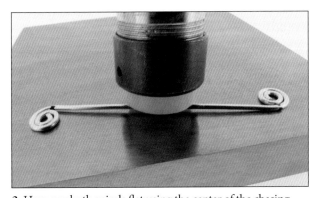

3. Hammer both spirals flat using the center of the chasing hammer's flat face. To harden the center of the shape without flattening it, gently tap a nylon-head mallet along the whole length of the wire. This will require more strikes than flattening the wire did. Test the rigidity of the wire at intervals and stop when you feel resistance to bending.

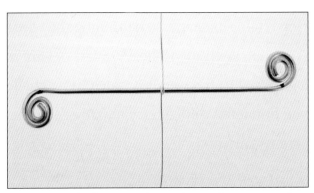

4. Cut 40" (1m) of 26-gauge (0.4mm) wire. Center it over the ring band and wrap it around once.

 Always form a ring smaller than the actual size to allow for springback of the wire. It is much easier to increase rather than decrease ring size.

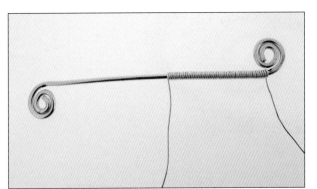

5. Hold the wire tail firmly while you wind the wrapping wire over, around, and back up again tightly to secure. The first few wraps are the most difficult, and it's important to make sure they are tight and perpendicular to the base wire. Hold the wire between your thumb and index finger close to the work. Treat the wire as if it were a piece of string and pull it tight. Don't worry; it won't break.

Continue wrapping toward the spiral on the right until you reach it. Every four wraps, tighten the work by pushing the coils together. Be careful not to wrap over the previous coil.

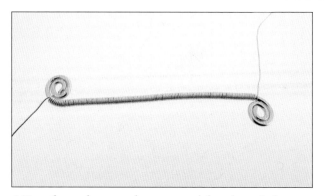

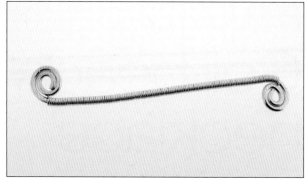

6. Turn the work over and wrap toward the other spiral.

7. On both ends, trim the wire on the inside of the spiral.

TIP

Don't worry if you don't have a ring mandrel. Look around the house for a hard cylinder about the diameter of your finger. Wrap your strip of paper around it to check the size; the mandrel should be slightly smaller.

8. To form the ring, place the center at one size smaller than the desired size. Hold with your thumb while pushing the ends toward each other around the mandrel with the thumb and index finger of the other hand. Fit the ring on your finger and readjust if necessary.

9. Tweak the spirals very slightly with flatnose pliers so they are in line with the ring and don't dig into your finger.

ANOTHER IDEA

Make this lovely

Celtic-look bangle to match your ring. Measure your wrist and add 10" (25cm) or 5" (12.5cm) for each spiral.

PROJECT22
Coil beads necklace

Coil beads require a lot of wire and patience, but it is well worth the effort: They bring lovely dimension to your jewelry. This project is versatile enough to make it your own by varying the size of the mandrels and wires, the wire colors, and the lengths and number of coils.

Length: 20½" (52cm)

WHAT YOU'LL NEED

- 5½' (1.7m) 18-gauge (1mm) wire
- 6' (1.8m) 22-gauge (0.6mm) wire (I used copper)
- 40' (12m) 26-gauge (0.4mm) wire
- 38mm focal bead
- **13** 8mm beads
- **22** 4mm round copper beads
- Mandrel: knitting needle, US size 2 (UK 12/2.75mm)
- Wire cutters
- Chainnose pliers
- Flatnose pliers
- Roundnose pliers
- Bench block
- Chasing hammer
- **2** 12mm GBs

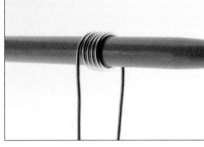

1. Cut 40" (1m) of 26-gauge (0.4mm) wire (or work from the spool). Leaving a small tail, make several counterclockwise coils to anchor the wire to the mandrel. Coil the remainder of the wire tightly clockwise. Work close to the end of the mandrel but avoid coiling on the tapered end. Move the work up as you need to and, every so often, push the coils together tightly. Coil for 2" (5cm). Remove the coil from the mandrel and trim the ends close to the coil.

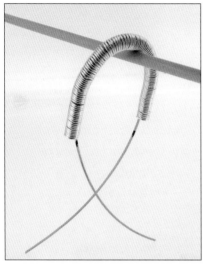

2. Clean and straighten a 6" (15cm) piece of 22-gauge (0.6mm) wire. Mark 2" (5cm) from each end. With your fingers, curve the wire in a U shape. Thread the coil on the curved inner-core wire and slide it to the center of the wire. Place the curved wire on the mandrel as shown.

3. This part is a little tricky; use a light touch. Hold one end of the inner-core wire in each hands and wrap the coil in opposite directions around the mandrel. The coiled wire will distribute itself evenly as you wrap. If the mandrel doesn't stay in place, wedge it between books (or even between your knees!)

4. Wrap each end in turn until you reach the inner-core wire. Make three tight wraps with the inner-core wire and trim. Make a total of 12 coiled beads. Use 18-gauge (1mm) wire and the 12mm GB to transform them into bead links. Make the central dangle in a similar way using 3½" (9cm) of wire for the inner core, but on one end, string an 8mm bead and make a spiral below the bead.

 TIP You have three wires to play with, so you can make an endless variety of different looks by changing the combinations of colors, gauges, materials, and mandrel sizes.

5. To make the loop part of the toggle clasp, cut 4" (10cm) of 18-gauge (1mm) wire. String a 12mm GB, bend the wire, and make a loop. String an 8mm bead up to the loop. Bend the wire at a right angle below the bead.

6. Place the bead on top of the widest part of a fine-point permanent marker and make a loop around the pen. Wrap once below the bead. Remove the work from the pen and hammer both loops flat. Make a spiral with the end of the wire and center it under the bead.

7. To make the toggle, cut 3½" (9cm) of 18-gauge (1mm) wire. String a 12mm GB, bend the wire, and make a loop. Using the tip of the roundnose pliers, bend the wire at a right angle below the loop. Measure and mark ½" (13mm) from the bend.

Parts of a coil bead

Three separate wires are needed to make a coil bead. **The coil** is usually the thinnest wire, which is wrapped around a mandrel. You can use sewing needles, large-gauge wire, nails, or knitting needles as mandrels, depending on the effect you want to achieve. **The inner core** is the wire you slip inside the finished coil to stabilize it. It must not be too thick or too hard because you have to work it without tools. Always cut more than you think you need because the coil will stretch in size. The inner core is also wrapped around a mandrel and secured at both ends. The mandrel can be a different size from that used to make the coil. **The core wire** is put through the coiled bead, which then can be treated like any normal bead for the purpose of attaching it to other components.

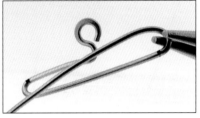

8. Make a hairpin bend using the tip of the roundnose pliers on the first mark. Mark 1" (2.5cm) from the bend and make a second bend. The shape should look like a mini clothes hanger.

9. Use the tip of the flatnose pliers to squash both ends of the toggle. Hammer the ends and the loop flat.

ANOTHER IDEA

Large, angular
beads contrast nicely with the spiral, curved look of coiled beads.

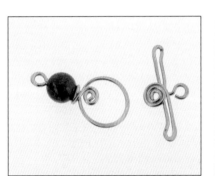

10. Measure 1½" (4cm) from the end of the wire toward the toggle and trim. Make a spiral, stopping in the center.

11. Cut 3" (8cm) of 18-gauge (1mm) wire. Make a figure 8 at one end, taking the length of the wire through the center of the shape. Hammer the loops of the 8. String a metal bead, the focal bead, a metal bead, and a 12mm GB. Trim and make a loop below the focal bead.

12. String a metal bead, an 8mm bead, and a metal bead on 18-gauge wire and make a loop on each end to make a bead link; make a total of 10 bead links. Make one bead link without metal beads. Start from the center to assemble: Link three coil beads and then on each side an 8mm bead link and a coil bead four times. Attach the plain bead link and toggle on one side and the toggle loop on the other. Attach the dangle to the focal bead. Attach a bead link to each side of the pendant's figure 8 and to the coil beads on either side of the central coil bead.

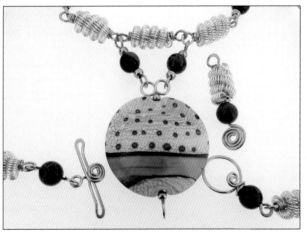

PROJECT23
Apple tree pendant

Trees are such a wonder of nature. They beautify our environment while giving us shelter, nourishment, warmth, oxygen, and a sense of stability and strength. The motif of this pendant is often called "the tree of life," and you'll see it carried out in many different ways. My sample shows a neat and tidy tree that I worked from top to bottom. Because trees are organic, there are no rules about how your tree should look. Make the twists loose rather than tight, gnarl and bend the trunk, add more branches, vary the branch sizes, add beads to the roots… the variations are endless after you have learned the basics.

Diameter: 1½" (4cm)

WHAT YOU'LL NEED

- 10" (25cm) 18-gauge (1mm) wire
- 4½' (2.6m) 26-gauge (0.4mm) wire
- **80** small chips and/or beads (no larger than 4mm)
- 1⅜" (4cm) mandrel
- Wire cutters
- Chainnose pliers
- Flatnose pliers
- Roundnose pliers
- Nylon-jaw pliers
- Bench block or anvil
- Chasing hammer
- 14mm GB

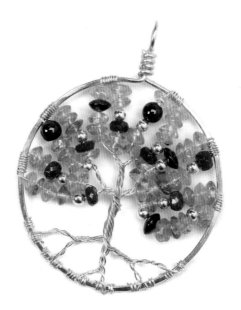

1. Clean and straighten the 18-gauge (1mm) wire piece. Place the GB on the end, bend at a right angle, and make a loop. Place the tip of the flatnose pliers below the loop and make a right angle bend as shown. The loop will be the bail of the pendant—just twist the loop a quarter-turn with flatnose pliers when the pendant is finished.

2. Hold the loop with your fingers and wrap the wire tightly around the mandrel. Loop the wire around the base of the stem.

3. Wrap about four times around the stem. If you find it difficult to wrap the wire with your fingers, use chainnose pliers for more strength. Work slowly and keep the work on the mandrel to avoid distorting the circular frame. Trim the wire. Remove the frame from the mandrel. Hammer the frame and the loop to flatten and harden the wire.

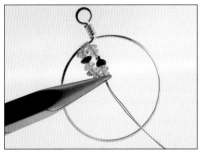

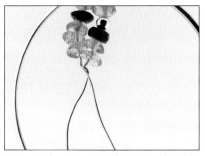

4. Cut six 9" (23cm) pieces of 26-gauge (0.4mm) wire. Loosely bend each wire in half; do not pinch or flatten the bend. Hook one piece on the frame near the loop and make six tight coils around the frame. To wrap in an enclosed space, push the part of the wire closest to the coil through the frame in a round shape. Imagine making a soap bubble (placing your index finger under the wire will make sure it stays round) and then pull the rest of the wire free. Wrap around the frame by smoothing it on with your finger.

5. This coiled wire is the start of a bead cluster. String five or six beads on each wire. Push the beads up to the frame. Hold the wires together with the tip of the chainnose pliers.

6. Twist the wires together twice, loosely or tightly depending on the look you like. Make two more bead clusters on the left and three on the right.

In this design, I cascaded down to a single root, but for a much quicker result and a more organic look, coil several wires at the same time around the frame. You can also kink the trunk and roots with chainnose pliers.

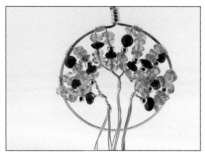

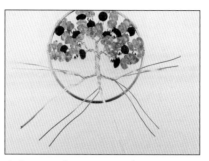

7. Twist together the stems of the two central clusters and then the two side clusters. You now have three stems instead of six.

8. Bring all the stems together and twist once or twice. Leave at least ⅜" (1cm) free to make the roots. Trim the stems so they are all the same size, leaving about 1" (2.5cm).

9. Separate the wires into three groups of four and twist each group twice. Separate each twisted stem into eight groups of two.

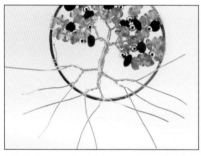

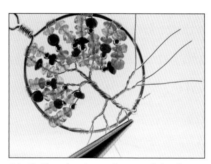

10. Twist together the two wires of each of the eight groups. Separate the 12 wires.

11. Coil each wire end around the frame several times. Use chainnose pliers to pull the wire tight.

12. The best place to trim the wires so they do not scratch the wearer is on the inside of the frame toward the front of the work. Trim each end, and then tuck and flatten each end with the tip of the chainnose pliers. Run your finger on both sides of the frame. If you can still feel a wire end, pull it out with chainnose pliers and trim and smooth the end again.

ANOTHER IDEA

Experiment with
various frame shapes and try using different types of beads.

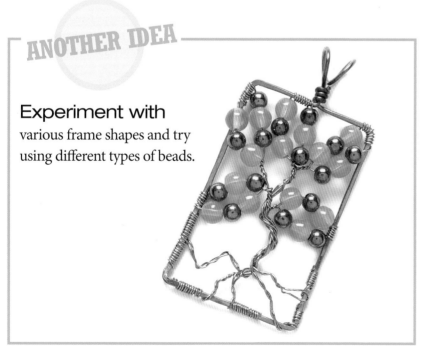

PROJECT24
Flower hair jewel

Width: 3¼" (8cm)

WHAT YOU'LL NEED

- 10' (3m) 26-gauge (0.4mm) wire
- Hair comb
- **5** 14mm coin-shaped beads
- **10** 10mm coin pearls
- **18** 8–10mm teardrop-shaped beads
- **3** 6mm pearls (flattened rounds)
- Wire cutters

I often create tiaras and hair combs for weddings, and I can spend many happy hours tweaking the wires so they look perfect from every angle. To make these flowers, look for coin-shaped beads to use for the outer layer of petals. All the beads must have holes that run along their lengths rather than being "top-drilled" (having a hole that goes from one side to the other at the top). I used a 2¾" (7cm) metal comb, but you'll find it fairly easy to adapt the design to a different size.

1. Cut 20" (50cm) of wire. String a teardrop-shaped bead pointed end first, leaving a 6" (15cm) tail. Mold the wire against the bead. Wrap the long end of the wire around the tail twice clockwise.

2. To make a second petal, string another teardrop pointed end first. Leave about ⅛" (3mm) of wire between the petals. Mold the wire against the back of the bead and wrap twice away from you.

TIP Resist the temptation to tweak the beads into place before the comb is completely finished. Twisting the wires more than necessary will weaken them and could even lead to breakage, so wait until the end to inspect the comb and make the last adjustments.

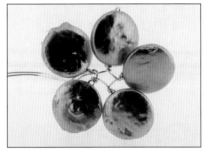

3. Make four more petals in this way. Always add the new bead to the left and wrap in the same direction. When the last bead is wired, take the wire under the flower to the gap between petals on the opposite side. String a 6mm pearl and bring the pearl and wire over the center to meet the tail wire.

4. Pull the two wires to the back of the work. Use the tips of your thumb and index fingers to grasp them tightly near the base of the flower and twist twice.

5. Make a five-petal shape with coin pearls following steps 1 and 2. These petals will not sit next to each other, but will overlap slightly.

ANOTHER IDEA

Mount flowers

on a hair elastic or hairpin instead of a comb. You can also use only the inner flower mounted on a hair elastic and wear a few of them dotted in your hair—a very popular look for brides.

6. String the inner flower wires through the hole in the middle of the five-petal shape. Gather all four wires close to the base. Hold them with your fingertips and twist twice.

7. Make a total of two side flowers and one center flower. Cut the tails to approximately 4" (10cm).

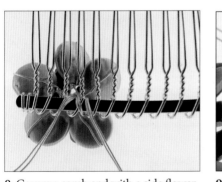

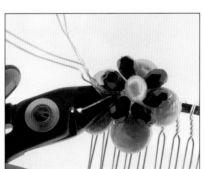

8. Covers a comb end with a side flower. String all four tail wires through the comb teeth. Split the wires into two sets. Wrap one set several times to the left and the other set to the right. Wrap each set around the flower base once in opposite directions.

9. Bring the wires up through the flower and trim. Tuck the wire ends well inside the flower. Wire the other side flower and, finally, the center flower in the same way.

PROJECT25
Masterpiece charm bracelet

Length: 7½" (19cm)

WHAT YOU'LL NEED

• 7' (2m) 18-gauge (1mm) wire
• 4' (1.2m) 20-gauge (0.8mm) wire
• 40" (1m) 22-gauge (0.6mm) wire
• 53' (16m) 26-gauge (0.4mm) wire
• 14' (4m) 28-gauge (0.3mm) wire
• Various sizes of beads
• ⅜" (9.5mm) mandrel
• Wire cutters
• Bentnose pliers
• Chainnose pliers
• Flatnose pliers
• Roundnose pliers
• Bench block and guard
• Chasing hammer
• Nylon-head mallet
• 12mm GB

Like a filmmaker's most spectacular work that caps a brilliant career, this final project incorporates nearly all the techniques of the craft you have learned and expands on them. This can truly be your masterpiece. I purposefully left the specifics of the beads and wire colors up to you—let your imagination run free to invent and add other dangles and use other gauges, shapes, or materials to make it your own.

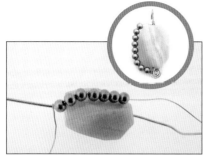

The charms

My Fair Lady String a large bead on 3" (7.5cm) of 18-gauge (1mm) wire. Using 26-gauge (0.4mm) wire, make several wraps at one end of the bead, string several metal beads, wrap it around the 18-gauge wire at the other end of the large bead, and trim. Make a spiral at one end of the 18-gauge wire. Slide the bead against it and make a loop using the 12mm GB at the other end.

La Dolce Vita Cut 6" (15cm) of 18-gauge (1mm) wire. Make a small loop at one end. Cut a comfortable length of 26-gauge (0.4mm) wire. About 2" (5cm) from one end, wrap several times around the 18-gauge wire close to the loop. String a small bead, make 10 close wraps with the wire tail, push the bead and the coil close to the loop, and trim. Continue adding beads in this way, wrapping tightly 10 times between beads. After the sixth bead, wrap for about 3" (8cm). Starting with the small lopp, make a spiral with the entire beaded and wrapped wire, placing roundnose pliers through the loop to start the spiral and continuing the shape using your fingers. Make a loop for attaching the charm to the bracelet.

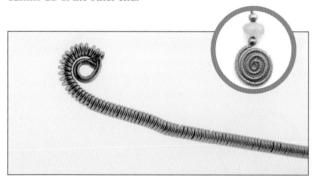

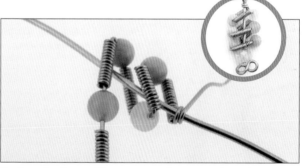

Funny Girl Make a P loop on one end of 5" (12.5cm) of 20-gauge (0.8mm) wire. Wrap 26-gauge (0.4mm) wire for 3" (8cm). Push the coil close to the loop. Start a spiral with roundnose pliers and then use flatnose pliers very gently to continue the shape. Straighten the neck. String your chosen beads and make a loop.

Back to the Future Using a piece of 18-gauge (1mm) wire as a mandrel, make a 2½" (6.5cm) coil with 26-gauge (0.4mm) wire. Remove the coil from the mandrel and cut it into seven pieces, each ¼" (6mm) long. Cut 6" (15cm) of 22-gauge (0.6mm) wire. String on a pattern of a coil and a 4mm bead six times, and string a coil. Secure the wire tail on 3" (8cm) of 18-gauge (1mm) wire. Wrap the coils and the beads around the wire, aligning the beads. Wrap the other end of the 22-gauge (0.6mm) wire to secure. String a bead on the 18-gauge wire and make a headpin ending (such as this figure 8). Make a loop at the other end.

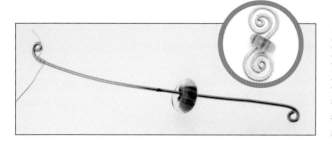

Mamma Mia! For this charm, choose a bead with a very large hole. Cut 4" (10cm) of 18-gauge (1mm) wire. Slide the bead onto the wire. Make a P loop at each end, facing the loops in opposite directions. Coil 26-gauge (0.4mm) wire starting near one loop, pass the wire through the bead hole, and coil to the other end. Mark the center. Make a double spiral as in Project 7, p. 36. Add a jump ring to attach.

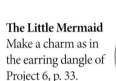

True Grit Cut 4" (10cm) of 20-gauge (0.8mm) wire as the core and mandrel. Make a 2" (5cm) coil bead as in Project 22, p. 80, with 28- (0.3mm) and 22-gauge (0.6mm) wire. Center the completed coil on the inner core wire and secure at both ends. Form the drop shape on a small cylinder (a pencil, for instance). Bend one wire up and the other at a right angle, wrap the neck, and trim. Make an open loop.

Fantasia This is a challenging double-wrapped coil that requires four wires. Make a 6" (15cm) coil with 28-gauge (0.3mm) wire on an 18-gauge (1mm) wire mandrel. Slip the coil on 12" (30cm) of 22-gauge (0.6mm) wire. Wrap around the same mandrel and secure at both ends. Remove from the mandrel. String and center the coil on 5" (13cm) of 22-gauge (0.6mm) wire. Bend the shape in the middle and coil around 3" (8cm) of 18-gauge (1mm) wire. Finish the bead at both ends.

The Love Bug Mark 6" (15cm) of 20-gauge (0.8mm) wire at 2½" (6cm). Coil with 28-gauge (0.3mm) wire from the mark for 2" (5cm). In the center of the coiled section, make a heart shape as in Project 18, p. 69. Wrap to secure. At the base of the heart, string beads on the 20-gauge wire and make a loop.

Fatal Attraction Make two caged beads as in Project 16, p. 63, and link them.

The Little Mermaid Make a charm as in the earring dangle of Project 6, p. 33.

Mary Poppins String a bead on 4" (10cm) of 18-gauge (1mm) wire and make flattened squiggles on each end.

Tangled Make a heart headpin, string a bead, and add a coiled bead. String a metal spacer and make a loop.

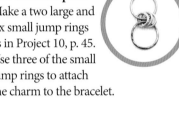

The Spiral Staircase Cut 3" (8cm) of 18-gauge (1mm) wire. Make a folded headpin end. String a metal bead and three small beads. Make a coil long enough to cover the small beads (about three times the combined width of the beads). Wrap one end of the coil's inner core wire next to the metal bead and wrap the coil around and between the beads. Secure the coil with several wraps. String a metal bead and make a loop with the 18-gauge wire.

The Usual Suspects Make a two large and six small jump rings as in Project 10, p. 45. Use three of the small jump rings to attach the charm to the bracelet.

TIP Lay all the dangles side by side before attaching them. Pay attention how they look together. For example, vary the lengths, widths, and bead positions so the whole looks harmonious.

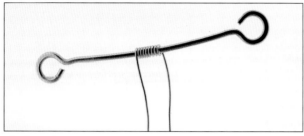

The bracelet

Each link is about ⅝" (1.5cm) long. Measure your wrist to determine how many links you need to make, and keep in mind that links are easy to add or remove. For each link, flush-cut 2¼" (5.6cm) of 18-gauge (1mm) wire. Using a 12mm GB, make a loop at both ends facing opposite directions. Hammer both loops flat with the chasing hammer. Strike the rest of the wire with the nylon-head mallet to harden. Wrap 26-gauge (0.40mm) wire in a tight coil around the core wire from loop to loop. Shape the wrapped core wire around the mandrel tightly .

For the clasp, cut 3½" (9cm) of 18-gauge (1mm) wire and wrap 26-gauge (0.4mm) around it tightly for 1¼".

ANOTHER IDEA

Any of the dangles

can be replicated to make earrings. Or have a go at designing some new dangles! You may have noticed that most of these dangles are dimensional rather than flat, so keep balance in mind as you design your own shapes.

How about turning your masterpiece into a real heirloom by making it in sterling silver?

Sit back and admire.
Look how far your wirework skills have come!

PROJECT 26
Embellished earring wires

This design is so versatile, these may be the only earring wires you will ever need. You can easily interchange the dangles. One pair with several dangles makes an impressive gift. I made the inner flower from Project 24 in four colors; just slip a small jump ring in one of the petals before wrapping it. In an hour, you can have an entire bouquet for your ears. How cool is that?

WHAT YOU'LL NEED

- 7" (9cm) 20-gauge (0.8mm) wire
- Wire cutters
- Flatnose pliers
- Roundnose pliers
- Bench block
- Chasing hammer
- Wire rounder
- File or emery board

Earring wires

Earring wires require very little time and effort to make and can be shaped in many lovely ways. Because earring wires actually go through flesh, it's important to pay attention to the materials you use and how you finish them.

- Some metals (especially nickel) can cause an allergic reaction. Copper usually doesn't, but it can turn earlobes green.
- The gauge must not be too thick so it can go through the ear easily. I suggest using 20-gauge (0.8mm).
- The ends must be absolutely rounded and smooth.
- The stem must be long enough to stay in the pierced ear but short enough for comfort.
- Avoid using very heavy beads, which are uncomfortable and pull the earlobe down. If you want big statement earrings, consider using beads made of lighter materials such as acrylic or aluminum.

1. Cut 3½" (9cm) of wire and mark it at 1½" (4cm). Make a spiral up to the mark and hammer the spiral flat. Place roundnose pliers on the mark and make a U shape as shown. Shape the curve of the earring wire over the mandrel.

2. Grasp the whole spiral in the tip of the flatnose pliers and swivel it to center it on the wire. Adjust and straighten the loop under the spiral. Place the curved part of the earring wire on the bench block and flatten it with the hammer. Use flatnose pliers to bend the very tip of the wire at a 30-degree angle. Smooth the end with a wire rounder and a file.

PROJECT 27
Double-ended clasp

Here is a new take on an old shape. This useful clasp, which can be opened from both ends, finishes a beaded link necklace with a balanced, symmetrical touch. Choose a small but sturdy bead—you push the wire against it with a fair amount of force.

WHAT YOU'LL NEED

- 4 x 8mm rondelle
- 4" (10cm) 18-gauge (1mm) soft wire
- Wire cutters
- Bentnose wire
- Roundnose pliers
- Bench block
- Chasing hammer

Clasps

Clasps enable a piece of jewelry to be opened and closed so the piece is held securely no matter how many movements the wearer makes. If you have ever lost a piece of jewelry due to a poorly made clasp, you will understand the importance of a well-designed and secure clasp.

A clasp should always:
- hold its shape, so the gauge and temper of the wire must be chosen carefully.
- be in proportion to the rest of the piece. Heavy beads require a strong clasp; delicate wirework, a daintier clasp.
- be appropriate to its use. Bracelets require the most secure clasps of all because they take more abuse than any other type of jewelry.
- be easy to open and close with smooth action.
- be deep enough not to slip off.
- be comfortable to wear. It should not catch on clothing or hurt the wearer in any way.

In addition, both parts of a clasp need to have harmony in proportion and design. Always think of the clasp as an integral, perhaps even focal, part of the design and not an afterthought.

TIP

Made the small loop the wrong way up? No problem. Grasp the loop in the pliers and twist it into the right position. This also works to change the orientation of spirals.

Cut 4" (10cm) of 18-gauge (1mm) soft wire and slide the bead to the center. Use your fingers to bend the wires closely around the bead in opposite directions.

With the tip of the bentnose pliers, bend both wires at a right angle.

Measure both ends and trim them to equal lengths (about 1¼"/3.2cm works well). Make a small upward loop at each end. On each end, measure ½" (1.2cm) from the bead, place roundnose pliers on the mark, and bend the wire over. Hammer the curve flat.

PROJECT 28
Cord bail and ends

Sometimes a focal bead is so outrageously gorgeous that you simply want to suspend it from a cord or ribbon. This bail is perfect for the job, and the easy-to-make cord ends and a clasp of your choice finish the look nicely.

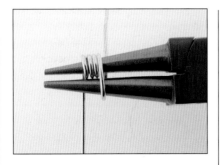

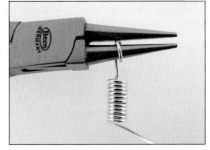

Bail

Cut 10" (25cm) of wire and mark the centerpoint. Place the wire on the mandrel and make three tight wraps to anchor it. Remove the wire from the mandrel. Place one jaw of the roundnose pliers through the coil and the other under it. Wrap the wire over the lower jaw, bring the wire back over the top jaw, and remove the coil. Place the coil on the mandrel and finish wrapping, making the same number of wraps on both ends. Trim the ends in a wedge, file, and use the pliers to tighten them against the coil. An option: Make a tiny spiral at each end of the wire.

Cord ends

Cut 8" (20cm) of wire and coil both ends of the wire on the mandrel until you have 1" (2.5cm) of straight wire remaining. Use flatnose pliers to make a right angle bend on one end. Trim the straight end to 1".

Measure 1" and cut. Place the coil on one jaw of the roundnose pliers and mark the pliers at the point where the coil rests (this marks the diameter of the coil).

Grasp the end of the wire at this point and make a double loop (like a mini coil). Continue rotating until the loop reaches the long coil.

On the other end, coil until you reach your desired length. Trim the wire. Place one cord end inside the coil and squeeze the end coil in the jaws of the flatnose pliers to secure the cord, being careful not to distort the rest of the coil. Pull the cord to check that it is held securely. String the bail. Make and attach a second cord end.

Pro tips

Now that you're an experienced wireworker, I'll share a variety of professional secrets to help you continue to master and enjoy the craft. Consider it my graduation gift!

Hammering tips

The hammer allows you to work-harden, strengthen, and embellish your wire creations. To hammer effectively, the first thing you need to do is *relax*. I often see students gripping their hammers with white knuckles as if their lives depended on it—all the while giving the wire timid little taps. Direct your energy at the hammer head, not the hammer grip. Hold the hammer at the bulb or at the end of the handle and deliver sharp, well-aimed blows.

Save your fingertips—use transparent packaging tape to hold tiny pieces to the bench block as you strike them.

Check your hammer head regularly. Scratch marks and nicks will transfer to your wire, so keep it nicely polished by filing and sanding if necessary.

Tool marks

First of all, stop worrying about tool marks. A lot of them will disappear with practice. Some marks are inevitable and add authenticity to a handmade piece. That said, you can minimize tool marks. Here are some tips.

Use a lighter grip on pliers. That "death grip" will eventually lessen of its own accord. As you become more experienced and at ease with your tools, you will learn to use the minimum force required to accomplish a task.

Use the correct tool for the job. It is sometimes tempting to use the closest at hand. For instance, after making a loop with roundnose pliers, straightening or opening the loop with the same pliers will almost certainly result in a mark. Use flatnose pliers instead.

Get rid of nicks and burs on your tools as soon as they appear. File and sand the surfaces smooth. In extreme cases, particularly if the jaws of pliers become misaligned, you may need to invest in a new tool.

Some pliers' sides can have a sharp edge that marks the wire every time. Don't hesitate to sand these edges until they are rounded; it's very common for jewelers to customize their tools.

If tool marks still bother you, wrap your pliers' jaws with tape or use a liquid silicone coating called Tool Magic to put a soft barrier between your pliers and the wire. These barriers have to be replaced frequently and you lose close contact with your wire, but they are effective at preventing marks.

Finally, for a professional finish:
- Check that every loop is straight and fully closed.
- Check that every wire end is filed and safely tucked away.
- Check for broken or cracked beads. It's rare, but it happens—and it compromises the whole piece.
- Run the tips of your fingers over your entire work to check for burs. Your fingers will always be more accurate than your eyes in this task.
- Wear the piece for a couple of hours. Any fault will quickly become apparent.
- Give your jewelry a final polish with a polishing cloth.
- Store each piece separately in an airtight bag with an anti-tarnish strip or a piece of chalk. Replace the strip or chalk several times a year.

About the author

Martine Callaghan has been passionate about wirework for more than 10 years, ever since she took her first certified college course in jewelry making. In 2005, she launched a full-time career in jewelry, creating and selling unique, handcrafted pieces, including a popular line of custom-made bridal jewelry, and creating educational tutorials. In 2009, she was named "Jewellery Maker of the Year in Wirework" by the UK magazine *Beads & Beyond*. She is the magazine's resident expert on wireworking, contributing a monthly column and answering readers' queries through the magazine's website. Martine lives in Edinburgh, Scotland.

Acknowledgments

I would like to thank my editor, Mary Wohlgemuth, for giving me this fantastic opportunity and believing in me. I am also grateful for the unwavering support and encouragement of my indulgent husband, John, my wonderful daughters, Marianne and Amanda, and my two generous sons-in-law, Lee and Chris. I am very fortunate to have an amazing family, and I dedicate this book to five very precious people: Dylan, Callum, Daniel, Emily, and Sophie, my adorable grandchildren, who keep me young and up to date!